Grimoire

Muerte, Volume 2

Altars, Meditations, Divination and Witchcraft Rituals for Devotees of Most Holy Death

Sophia diGregorio

2016
Winter Tempest Books

DEDICATION

This book is dedicated to all those who dare to explore the true nature of reality.

CONTENTS

Author's Note   vii

Introduction: A Deeper Exploration of the
Occult Powers of Santa Muerte   1

**Part 1. The Altar: A Generator and
Accumulator of Santa Muerte's Power**

1   The Altar of Santa Muerte: Its Purpose and   5
   How to Use It

2   Powerful Meditations for Charging the Altar
   and Other Objects of Santa Muerte's Power   19

3   Gemstone Correspondences to Santa Muerte's
   Powers   33

4   The Influence of Numerology on the Altar   47

5   Altar Arrangements for Various Purposes with   53
   Prayers

Part 2. The Occult Powers of Santa Muerte

6   Three Rituals to Communicate with the Dead   81

7   Divination with Santa Muerte   89

8   Rituals to Develop Your Occult Powers and Achieve High Spiritual States   99

9   Rituals and Talismans to Influence the Weather   113

10   Transcendence: Encouragement and a Warning   119

  Appendix   125

AUTHOR'S NOTE

In this second volume, I share with you my own personal methods for working with Santa Muerte, which you may use and adapt to your own devotion to her. The procedures for invoking her powers through meditation and ritual, as I describe in this book, have proven very effective for me and have led to remarkable personal experiences.

I hope the information in this book helps you to have your own amazing personal experiences with Santa Muerte. May your relationship with her bring you peace, healing, knowledge, personal power, and ultimately all the things you desire.

Sophia diGregorio

A DEEPER EXPLORATION OF THE OCCULT POWERS OF SANTA MUERTE

While the first volume of this series, *Grimoire of Santa Muerte: Spells and Rituals of Most Holy Death, the Unofficial Saint of Mexico*, provides an introduction to Santa Muerte and her contemporary devotion, this second volume further explores her occult powers. In this one, you will learn how to increase your personal power, psychic abilities, powers of divination, and skill performing acts associated with traditional witchcraft with her assistance.

Among the topics explored in this book is that of the altar as a center of Santa Muerte's power. It provides techniques for increasing your vital force, generating and manipulating energy, charging the altar and the objects on it, and storing this power until you are ready to use it for a particular purpose. It discusses statues and talismans as energy accumulators, which make the altar's energy portable, as well as other methods of directing the power of the altar, including the use of gemstones in correspondence with Santa Muerte's various powers. It shows how numerology and geometric formations may be used to increase and direct energy on the altar.

You will learn how Santa Muerte can assist you in the acquisition of knowledge from both mundane and spiritual sources. She can help you to develop your psychic abilities and divination skills so that you may look into the future to see what events may occur and how to intervene, if necessary. You will learn how to communicate directly with Santa Muerte, who quickly brings spirits of the dead and helps you connect with a variety of entities.

This volume includes rituals to break old mental programming about the nature of the world and to acquire traditional witchcraft abilities like those practiced both by Western Europeans and the Indians of the North American continent, involving such things as transmogrification, the projection of the astral and etheric bodies, energy transference, and weather control.

Santa Muerte is a very potent, primordial spirit of the Underworld whose purpose on earth is to help anyone who asks. She has many offices and aspects and is much more powerful, versatile and reliable than any other saint. Where other saints, gods or spirits fail, Santa Muerte consistently achieves fast, reliable results on behalf of her devoted children, which is why she is so very much loved and venerated by those who have experienced her power. Even those who remain faithful to the Church rely upon her for all their needs because she is so versatile and consistently brings results.

Devotion to Santa Muerte is a lifestyle based on experience with her abilities rather than blind faith. As she proves her power to you in a personal way, she naturally becomes a part of your daily life. By developing a close personal relationship with her, you will have access to her immense powers whenever you need it, bringing great success to your endeavors, whether they are of a spiritual or mundane nature.

PART 1.

THE ALTAR: A GENERATOR AND ACCUMULATOR OF SANTA MUERTE'S POWER

Sophia diGregorio

THE ALTAR OF SANTA MUERTE: ITS PURPOSE AND HOW TO USE IT

A triune of united forces makes witchcraft possible: Energy; will; and power.

Energy is the basis for the existence of the universe and everything in it. Essentially, nothing is inert matter at either the physical or metaphysical level; everything is comprised of vibrating energy of different degrees of density. Energy, rather than matter, is both what we use and what we influence when we practice witchcraft.

The **will** is an exertion of the energy of the mental body, which is one dimension of the entire auric field of the human body, to find resonance with the energy of the thing to be influenced in order to cause a change to occur in it according to the witch's desire. It is by means of the will that a witch steers energy in the direction he or she wants it to go.

In order for this action of the will to be very effective, it requires a great deal of **power**. This power may come from within the witch, either as a naturally large supply of the vital force or by acquisition of it through training. Another important source of the witch's power comes from working with very powerful spiritual allies. Santa Muerte is one of the greatest sources of this power.

As you work with her, you will come to know her in many different ways, including as a healer, a benefactor, an avenger, a source of inspiration and information, a liaison between the living and the dead, a provider and a peace maker. Her purpose is to help those who are in need. She will not assist you in doing evil, but she will help you with practically anything else you desire.

Santa Muerte is described by some as a "hungry spirit." Although it is true that she requires a lot of dedication, she rewards her devotees with great power and fast results. While she is easy to work with, there are basic rules for communicating with her and ways of increasing the availability of her power for your use. She responds best when she is not neglected, when her energy is regularly fed, most often upon an altar dedicated exclusively to that purpose.

How to Use the Altar: Energy Storage and Transference

In some modern forms of witchcraft, an altar is often regarded as an item to be decorated and admired. While it is a fine thing to have a tidy and neatly arranged altar, it should not be regarded as an item of household decor. A proper altar is never simply "decorated."

Far from being a static object to be admired, your altar to Santa Muerte is a dynamic device to be used as a center of her power and an instrument of your will. Every item that you place on it should have the purpose of accumulating, influencing and transmitting its energy.

When you arrange an altar to Santa Muerte, each item you place on it — the various types of images of her, other objects representing her power, candles, other offerings, and the colors and numbers of objects you use — imparts its own energetic frequencies to it. Together, they produce an energy harmonic similar to that of a musical chord. When you set up a proper altar arrangement, you create a system, which may be seen as an energetic matrix, for accomplishing a particular purpose.

Conducting a formal consecration ritual is just the beginning of the process of energizing the altar and other objects for the purpose of working with Santa Muerte. Whenever you repeatedly use an altar or an object like a statue or talisman, it begins to take on the energy characteristics of Santa Muerte and store this energy in its every atom. The connection between yourself, the object and the power of Santa Muerte flowing through it is strengthened by degrees. This energy is accumulated and concentrated in the object.

It becomes instantly available to you when you hold such a statue or talisman or when you go to your altar and place your hands upon it. Whenever you work with these objects, you change their subtle fields and tune them to resonate with your own energy. When the energy is sealed into a talisman or image of Santa Muerte, it may then be used to transfer energy to the person who wears it or holds it. The object will retain this energy and radiate it. The energy may, also, be mentally directed.

Whenever you make your invocations and prayers to Santa Muerte, lay your hands on the altar to create a conduit; this allows you to either charge the altar by projecting energy into it or to receive energy from it, as you will it. Regularly charge your altar to ensure that it will always be infused with a strong supply of Santa Muerte's power.

Statues and Talismans as Energy Accumulators and Transmitters

Once you determine the objective you want Santa Muerte to help you accomplish, set up the energy matrix of your altar according to your purpose, then feed its power with offerings, meditations, invocations and prayers. Each object and offering you place on the altar is not just symbolic of a particular type of energy, but actually possesses a particular metaphysical energetic quality.

The energy harmonic generated by the individual objects, their colors, their intrinsic qualities, their numbers and even their geometrical arrangement, all help to determine the nature and degree of power generated, accumulated and broadcast by the altar.

Not only your altar, but the statues, talismans and similar objects you use to connect with Santa Muerte, may be likened to solar energy accumulators or batteries that can be charged and recharged. Power is accumulated and stored in these objects so it is available when you are ready to use it.

When statues of different colors and iconographic representations of Santa Muerte are placed on the altar or used in meditation, they become accumulators and transmitters of those particular aspects of her power that they represent.

Talismans, including scapulars and images of Santa Muerte, carried or worn on necklaces and bracelets, may be used in the same fashion. They may be energized on the altar, their power stored and carried with you and refortified when you meditate with them.

In the same way, gemstones, especially carvings in the shape of skulls or owls may be used to enhance the energy of an altar for a specific purpose. They may, also, be used as accumulators of this energy and as sources of power according to their intrinsic metaphysical properties.

Meditating with these objects is a means of both charging them and receiving energy from them. Simply holding objects that have been previously charged this way transmits their specific energy to a person. Placing these same items on the altar energizes and intensifies its power.

Your altar to Santa Muerte acquires power, not from the physical matter of the objects and offerings on it, but from their metaphysical energy. The topic of charging images of Santa Muerte, talismans, and the entire altar is discussed in greater detail in the next two chapters.

The Power and Influence of Plants as Offerings

When they are used as offerings on the altar, plants and their particular parts, such as seeds, roots, flowers, or resins, produce metaphysical effects that are similar to their actions on the physical body. For instance, coffee speeds the digestive processes, moves obstructions out of the system, and energizes the physical body; similarly, when it is used on the altar, its metaphysical energy moves events along faster, destroys obstacles, and provides quick energy to your working.

Plants that you grow yourself make especially powerful offerings. As you plant them, tend them, and prepare to use them on the altar, speak to the spirit of the plants in a prayerful way. Tell them what you want them to do, what role they are to play in your ritual.

Plants may be offered live, freshly cut, or dried. Place a live plant in a small pot of dirt directly on the altar. Freshly cut herbs and flowers should be placed in a small vase. Their life force energy provides power to the altar and their metaphysical properties influence the energy there.

A small amount of dried herbs should be burned in a small cauldron or other fireproof container, which is placed on a tile or other high heat-safe surface. Think of this as a burnt offering, its smoke rising up to reach another realm, bringing with it your messages, prayers, and desires. Avoid the use of charcoal to burn dried herbs, resins, and other plant material. The charcoal is undesirable because it emits carbon monoxide fumes and changes the energy of the substance being burned. Generally, herbs are not burned on the altar to produce an aroma, but to release the metaphysical energy of the plant. Therefore, it is not necessary for it to burn for a long period of time.

Essential oils of appropriate plants may, also, be placed on the rim of 7-day candles or glass votive candleholders to influence their energy. Simply rub two or three drops of an oil on the rim before you light the candle.

Tobacco as an Offering

Tobacco is a versatile and powerful offering, which may be used for any purpose. Whether explicitly stated or not, it may be used in any ritual provided in this book. It is an especially powerful offering in rituals involving healing, prosperity, powerful protection, divination, spirit communication and expressions of gratitude. It may either be smoked in a cigarette or burned on the altar as a dried, loose herb.

Tobacco helps you achieve a deep trance state very quickly so that you can communicate with spirits and receive the answers you need about important matters. It has the power to connect you with the spiritual realms of the heavens, the underworld, and all the dimensions in between.

Like any powerful herb, it has powers to both heal and destroy depending upon how it is used. Take care not to abuse the spirit energy associated with this plant by using it recreationally.

Many devotees use commercial tobacco and while this is not wrong, the author recommends using the unprocessed, dried herb. Ideally, the tobacco you use as an offering to Santa Muerte should be very pure, especially in rituals for healing. Store-bought cigarettes contain tobacco with dangerous chemical additives and their filters contain microscopic fiberglass particles, which go into the atmosphere when they are smoked. These impurities and particles contain their own metaphysical energy, which may interfere with your work.

If you smoke unadulterated, loose tobacco for ritual purposes, do so in a pipe or in a self-rolled, unfiltered, cigarette, without inhaling the smoke directly into your lungs. You may blow the smoke across the altar and gently into the face of Santa Muerte as a means of connecting with her spirit. Alternatively, burn some dried tobacco in a small cauldron or censer and use a feather, which you have set aside expressly for ritual purposes, to direct the smoke across your altar.

When you grow, care for, and gather tobacco plants yourself, they become even more powerful. There are many different species of tobacco, which can be grown in a variety of climates and types of soil. Many North American Indians regard tobacco as the primary and the holiest of all plants, which possesses the spirit of the Creator.

Marijuana as an Offering

Marijuana has similar uses to tobacco on the altar. Like tobacco it has great powers, which can be used to heal or destroy, depending on how you focus its energy. Pure, unadulterated marijuana, especially that which you have grown, tended and harvested yourself with respect, is the most powerful.

The Western medical and governmental establishments have demonized both marijuana and tobacco and a culture of abuse has been created around them. But, in their pure forms, when they are used properly and respectfully, they are among the most versatile and powerful healing agents on the planet.

As always, be aware of the laws in your jurisdiction before choosing to make an offering of substances that might be government controlled, including tobacco, marijuana and other herbs.

How to Charge an Offering

Throughout this book, offerings for a particular ritual are suggested on the basis of the type of energetic influence required to best achieve the desired outcome. Examples of typical offerings include corn, coins, flowers, candles, incense, tequila, whiskey, water, salt, and herbs according to their metaphysical properties. By charging your offerings, you increase their inherent energy.

Before you perform a ritual, you may charge any of your offerings by placing them in an appropriate container for use on the altar, then making a sign of the cross over them and directing their powers by speaking to the plant spirit, telling it exactly what you want it to do for you in this situation. It's not necessary to charge candleholders or other vessels, however, such items may be consecrated or simply set aside solely for use on your altar.

To charge an offering, use the following procedure:

1. Hold the item in your left hand.

2. Make the sign of the cross over it, pointing with your index and middle fingers at the same time, as you say the following words:

By the elemental forces of fire (+), water (+), air (+), and earth (+), and in the name of Most Holy Death, I charge you that your intrinsic powers shall be multiplied in my service.

When you point your fingers this way to direct the energy, each finger naturally generates a charge similar to that of a battery; the index finger is positive and the middle finger is negative.

3. With your two fingers still pointed at the object, further direct the spirit (intelligent metaphysical energy) of the offering, by telling it what you want it to do for you. You are making a telepathic communication with the spirit, so you may do this silently or aloud, however you feel comfortable.

4. Then, place the object on the altar.

How to Cleanse Unwanted Energy from Objects

Cleanse new images and other ritual objects before placing them on the altar, not just to wipe away the physical dirt, but to cleanse unwanted metaphysical energy, which might interfere with your operation. Such items include: candleholders, bowls, plates, other vessels, incense burners, and altar cloths.

To cleanse both the physical dirt and old metaphysical energy from newly acquired items the traditional way, moisten a clean cloth with a few drops of whiskey and rub it over the object.

Alternatively, to quickly and simply cleanse the energy from items on your altar or to clear the energy of an entire altar, enter a meditative state, then make a few passes with your right hand palm down over the item using a motion away from you. See the unwanted subtle energy collecting in a ball, growing larger with each pass of your hand. Once you have collected the old energy, flick the ball away from you. See the ball of energy consumed in vibrant green flames. Repeat this procedure once or twice to cleanse a smaller object; perform it several times to energetically cleanse your entire altar.

After you have cleansed the object, you may consecrate it to the service of Santa Muerte. It is only necessary to perform a consecration ritual on an object one time. Afterward, a cleansing may performed on it whenever you feel the need to clear unwanted energy it has accumulated.

A simple way to consecrate an object is to make the sign of the cross over it as you say, "In the name of the Father, the Son and the Holy Ghost, I dedicate you to the service of Most Holy Death." A more complex ritual for the consecration of the altar, itself, is provided in the first volume of this series, entitled, Grimoire of Santa Muerte: Spells and Rituals of Most Holy Death, the Unofficial Saint of Mexico. Although, repeatedly using your altar and the items on it solely for Santa Muerte rituals will condition them to this purpose over time.

Handling Personal Effects

Never cleanse personal effects, which are items that contain the vibration of a person or entity you wish to do work on. Examples of personal effects include photographs of a person or place, hair, nail clippings, and blood. The energy of these items should be preserved as much as possible. When you collect or handle them, try not to contaminate their energy by touching them with your fingers.

To avoid contamination of these items, carefully collect them with tweezers or clean plastic gloves. Place the personal effect in a clean, new, white envelope. Store the envelope inside a plastic bag.

Removing Items from the Altar

Whenever you remove an object from the altar, perform a quick rite to direct the energy. If you want the energy to go entirely to the altar to be stored and accumulated for future used, direct it there; or, if you want it to go from the altar into an object, such as a talisman, direct it there. Seal the energy into the object, where it will remain until you are ready to use it.

To direct energy from an object to the altar, invoke and speak directly to the elemental forces of which the energy is comprised. As you make the sign of the cross over the object, say:

By the powers of the earth (+), by the force of fire (+), by the inspiration of air (+), and the virtues of water (+), seal the energy from this object into this altar.

Visualize the energy flowing from the object to be removed into the altar. You may use your hands to guide the flow of energy. Doing this helps you to move the energy with the elemental forces that flow through your own body and it helps you keep your mental focus.

Then, see it being sealed into the altar with your mind's eye. Visualize a ball of blue-tinged light surrounding the altar. This color has a natural stabilizing capacity at the astral and etheric levels. Afterward, remove the item from the altar.

When you do this, you are training your mental force (will) to focus on this energy and direct it. After you do it a number of times, making the sign of the cross each time, it becomes second nature.

After you become accustomed to doing this, you may further abbreviate this procedure by simply making the sign of the cross over the object with your two fingers. Then, visualize the energy going where you want it to go and remaining there, stabilized in a blue-tinged ball of light. This is an example of how ritual ultimately makes working with Santa Muerte and her metaphysical energy easier and more efficacious.

Conversely, when you want to energize an object from the altar that you plan to use elsewhere, such as a talisman to be used to transmit Santa Muerte's healing energy to a sick person, visualize the energy flowing from the altar into that object. Seal it there until it is ready to be used using the same words as above, except at the end say, "seal the energy from the altar into this object." The energy may be released, again, by your will. If the object is one to be given to a person for healing, instruct the energy that it is to release when the person who needs healing touches it.

At your discretion, you may eat from the altar. You may share part of your food with Santa Muerte as an offering or place food upon the altar for her blessing before you eat it. When you have finished with an offering, you may either consume some of it or bury it, so that it becomes part of the cycle of regeneration. Whenever you remove any food from the altar, perform a little rite, as described above, to direct the energy wherever it will best serve your purposes.

Dispose of the remains from the altar based on what they were used for. For example, it is not advised to eat offerings used in rituals for revenge, instead those remains should be disposed of at a location off your property. But, you might consume offerings that are used in a working for love, friendship, or prosperity.

How to Cultivate a Greater Awareness of the Energy

Be mindful of the flow of energy on the altar and within the items you place on it or remove from it. Allow yourself to see and sense the flow of this energy and direct it the way you want it to go. It has an intelligence that you can interface with using your mental force (will). You can direct it entirely mentally or by incorporating your hands and your words.

Practice increasing your awareness. To do this, hold an item from the altar that represents Santa Muerte's power. An ideal example of such an item is a resin image of Santa Muerte that is only a few inches tall. As you hold it with both hands, close your eyes and allow yourself to become aware of the subtle energy flowing through your body, through your hands, and through the item, itself. Do this for, at least, a minute.

Still holding this item in your left hand, make the sign of the cross over it using your two fingers, conscious, as you do so, that you are invoking the elemental forces of creation.

Now, hold this item between your two hands, again, and feel the flow of the energy. It flows through your hands very strongly now into the item and radiates outward from it. For a minute or two, keep your eyes closed and allow yourself to see this energy with your mind's eye. It is a large, vibrating, pulsating glob of energized etheric matter in your hands.

The more you do this, the more you tune your senses and the stronger your impressions become. When you can easily see and sense it, this energy is very easy to work with. It can be pushed or pulled by your hands and your mind. It can be made to move quickly and with impact or slowly and steadily. Speak to the energy in much the same way you might speak to a pet or a plant that you care for. Although it is not human or animal, the energy has a kind of intelligence of its own, so it will respond to your words.

The same way you can use your mental field (your mind) to directly influence the mental fields of others and tap into them for information, you are able to interface with your altar and the objects you use there. All things that exist in the physical world have metaphysical fields, even if they are not as sophisticated as those of humans and animals. They can be influenced by the mind and by energy projections from your own metaphysical bodies, which you direct by means your mental body (the force of your will).

Similarly, whenever you make the sign of the cross on yourself, don't just go through the motions, but allow yourself to feel and see the flow of energy throughout your body. When you make the Catholic-style sign of the cross, you activate important energy centers (chakras) in your body, signaling them to increase their energy flow and come together as one force flowing through you. Allow yourself to see and feel the energy center of the third eye, the heart center and two secondary energy centers located near your armpits, enlarging and increasing their flow of etheric energy.

When you touch your forehead and then touch your heart center, you are connecting the two basic elements, fire and water, to form an electric charge, initiating the sequence of the elements that comprise the creative force. See and feel the flow of this energy activated in the third eye and heart centers when you touch these areas and when you touch the two secondary centers near your armpits. Allow yourself to feel these energy centers become very active and energized. Feel the powerful flow of this elemental energy, which streams through the pathways of the cross, then grows into a pulsating ball of electrified, etheric power — its vibrational field so dense that it is very nearly physical — which surges through your arms into your hands and fingertips.

When you make the sign of the cross this way the words you use are less important than what you see, feel and experience when you do it. You may use these words: "*For thine (+) is the kingdom (+) and the power (+) and the glory [+] forever and ever*" or use other words that relate to your understanding of the elemental forces, if you deem them more suitable. Whatever words you choose, make a ritual of it and use it every time.

After you make the sign of the cross, say "*Amen.*" Then, put your palms and fingertips together in the classical prayer position to form a circuit of energy. At this point, if you pull your hands apart, you will likely feel a static-electrical energy between your palms, which you can direct any way you like.

When you do this invocation of the elemental energy, mindful of its flow, and then invoke the powers of Santa Muerte, you will likely feel a very strong sense of her presence around your altar. Often, it will be palpable. Working with the elemental forces lays the groundwork for a very strong energy field, which facilitates her power.

The information in the next few chapters is a guide to various influences, methods of increasing the power of the altar, and controlling the frequency harmonic it generates. Generating and directing energy on the altar by means of meditation is further discussed in the next two chapters. As you read the rest of this book, keep in mind the nature of energy, will, and power, as it pertains to your altar and your work with Santa Muerte.

POWERFUL MEDITATIONS FOR CHARGING THE ALTAR AND OTHER OBJECTS OF SANTA MUERTE'S POWER

Performing a meditation regularly while holding or touching an object associated with Santa Muerte's power is a means of charging it. You increase its power and your connection to it each time you meditate with it. When such regularly energized objects are placed on the altar, they enhance its power. Meditation can, also, be used as a direct means of charging the altar.

Meditating to charge an altar and its components is especially useful when you have a clear, singular purpose you want to accomplish, for instance, when you have a need for powerful protection, powerful healing, or great success, and you want to bend all your focus toward this end. It helps you to concentrate all the energy you can into your altar to Santa Muerte, with which you can accumulate, generate, and transmit her power.

The meditations provided in this chapter may be used whenever you want to invoke the powers of Santa Muerte and work with her, either at your altar or while resting, traveling or anytime when performing your usual rituals at your altar is not practical. They may, also, be used to invoke her powers in situations in which you have no room to create an altar or in living situations in which you must be discreet.

Conduct your meditations in a sitting, standing or lying down position while holding a statue or other object, such as one of the gemstones described in the next chapter, representing Santa Muerte's power.

Whenever you meditate, take, at least, two deep breaths and allow yourself to become very relaxed and go into a state which is near sleep, but in which you are still conscious. The state you must try to achieve is similar to the twilight you experience when initially falling asleep or first waking up; it is the moment when you are between the stages of consciousness and dreaming.

Basic Meditation to Charge Images of Santa Muerte

The Basic Meditation is focused on the Akashic field, the fundamental element out of which the other four elements and all things are formed. Black and purple are the two basic colors of Santa Muerte, which are indicative of her primordial nature. This primary meditation is very powerful and should precede any of the meditations on her various aspects, which are described further below, to strengthen them.

For meditation purposes, choose statues made of resin or other solid material instead of the hollow ones, which are very good for particular operations on the altar, but not durable enough to be held or carried very much. You may, also, use gemstone carvings of skulls or owls representing her powers according to their intrinsic metaphysical properties, as discussed in *Chapter 3. Gemstone Correspondences to Santa Muerte's Powers*.

Choose the color and type of Santa Muerte statue that best suits your purpose, for example, amber for healing, white for protection, black for the ultimate protection and revenge, gold for financial concerns, green for legal matters, red for love, and so on. The white Santa Muerte statue is considered neutral. A list of color associations for Santa Muerte may be found in the *Appendix*.

These color associations are ancient and almost universal. Similar ones may be found among the Indians of the North American continent, including the Mayans, the Aztecs, the Cherokee, the Navajos, as well as in the literature of the Buddhists and Hindus.

Some colors are common and very commercially available while others are somewhat rare. If you wish to change the color representation of your Santa Muerte statue, you may simply stitch a small hooded cape for her. Some resin statues are coated with acrylic paint, the color of which can be changed to suit your purpose.

Once you have selected an appropriate representation, perform the *Basic Meditation* to charge and energize your Santa Muerte image:

While holding the item, visualize a black ball of energy forming in the palms of your hands. Spend some time seeing this blackness accumulate in your hands where you are holding the image of Santa Muerte. After you have formed a dense, black ball, see it being energized by vibrant flashes of purple lightning. These flashes have an electric quality, which you can not only see with your minds eye, but you can clairaudiently hear and feel vibrating and pulsing in your hands and throughout your entire body.

Visualize this energy filling the object for several minutes. Complete the charging meditation by visualizing a blue-tinged ball of white light surrounding it, stabilizing this energy and sealing it into the object.

You may use this procedure to directly energize your entire altar, as well.

Basic Meditation to Charge the Altar

Stand before your altar, place your hands on it and form the ball of energy there just as you would if you were holding a smaller object in your hands. See the primordial energy in a black ball, charged with purple arcs of electricity, filling up every atom of the altar and the objects on it.

You may, also, perform this meditation while lying down across the room and projecting the formation of the energetic ball onto the altar. Mentally, see it growing, encompassing the altar and penetrating the objects there with popping, crackling primordial energy.

When you have finished, stabilize the energy you have placed there by visualizing the same blue-tinged ball of white light surrounding it.

This meditation may be regarded as another method of feeding the altar. It may be used in conjunction with your usual offerings or as a substitute for them at times when you are unable to maintain your altar the normal way.

Meditations for the Various Aspects of Santa Muerte

After you have completed the *Basic Meditation* with your image of choice, make the sign of the cross over the object to invoke the elements, as discussed in the previous chapter. Then, proceed with one of the following meditations according to your needs.

In every instance, when you meditate with Santa Muerte and invoke her powers, be as specific as possible about the nature of your problem and what outcome you wish to see. Recite the meditation and your desires, in the form of a petition, aloud or silently, whichever makes you feel more comfortable. Then, silently contemplate the outcome you desire, allowing yourself to strongly visualize, as if you were in a dream state, your desires coming to fruition.

When you are ready to end your session, stabilize the energy and seal it into the object by making the sign of the cross over it and visualizing the energy surrounding it in a ball of blue-tinged light.

If you perform these meditations while lying down, you might fall asleep. That is all right. Just continue the meditation when you awaken or at the next convenient opportunity.

Whenever you begin a new meditation session, perform the *Basic Meditation*, again, to enliven and invigorate the energy accumulating in the object.

Healing with the Amber or Orange Santa Muerte or the Santa Muerte Incarnate (Encarnada)

The amber aspect of Santa Muerte is for healing and breaking bad habits and addictions. Orange is a more rare color of Santa Muerte and while it is, also, used for healing, it is typically employed in rituals to energize and cleanse the physical body. Santa Muerte Incarnate is depicted with half the face and body of a beautiful, young vibrant woman in perfect health and the other half as a skull and skeleton, which represent Santa Muerte's ultimate healing abilities and her infinite power over both life and death. These representations of Santa Muerte are associated with miraculous healing.

Meditation of the Amber Santa Muerte or Santa Muerte Incarnate: *O Most Holy Death, I invoke thee and thy infinite power of healing. I ask that you use your power over life and death to heal this body. It is a miracle to some, but not to me, for I know your unlimited power and intelligence. That which is impossible to others is but a trifle for you. Bring your immense power to bear on this situation and allow healing to take place at once. Mend all that is broken in this body, rejuvenate, restore, and revivify it by the immense powers of your holy office, which exist outside of time and space.*

Meditation of the Amber Santa Muerte to Break a Bad Habit or Addiction: *O Most Holy Death, I invoke thee and thy infinite powers to intervene to break this harmful behavior pattern. Cleanse and purify this mind and body and strengthen the will and resolve of your devoted child.*

Meditation of the Orange Santa Muerte to Dispel Infection and Disease: *O Most Holy Death, I invoke thee and thy infinite powers of healing. I ask that you use your power over life and death to heal this body, which is burdened by disease. It is a miracle to some, but not to me, for I know your unlimited power and intelligence. That which is impossible to others is but a trifle for you. Cleanse and purify this body at once, so that it is free from all discomfort, infection and disease.*

Protection of Pregnant Women with the Santa Muerte with Child

The Santa Muerte with Child depicts the Santa Muerte with an embryo visible inside transparent resin. Use it for the protection of pregnant women and the unborn.

Meditation of the Santa Muerte with Child: *O Most Holy Death, I ask for your protection from all accidents, violence, envy and malice. Ward off all evil, ill will and hatred. Arrange for me a safe environment, preserve my health and my life and let my child be born healthy and strong.*

Total Protection, Revenge and the Release of Innocent Prisoners with the Black Santa Muerte

Black is the primordial color, which represents power, strong protection from enemies and revenge. The black Santa Muerte statue represents total protection from all enemies, both incarnate and discarnate. Use the black Santa Muerte when you have very dangerous or powerful enemies and must defy the authoritarian establishment to achieve justice or to obtain protection for yourself, your home, your family or your financial interests.

Meditation of the Black Santa Muerte for Total Protection and Revenge Against Powerful Enemies: *O Most Holy Death, I have confronted my own mortality and, by your blessing, I have lived and learned the immenseness of your power. Now and forevermore, you walk with me, Santa Muerte. You are with me when I eat, when I sleep and while I work. You watch over me and you guide me. Grant me the peace and privacy I need, so that I may accomplish my ends without fear of sabotage. By the power of your holy companion, the owl, give me the power to see evil where it lurks in the darkness. Cloak me in your holy mantle; let it be a shroud of protection to hide me from those who wish to harm me.*

O Holy Mother of Darkness, I have been denied justice in the past, but I know you will right this wrong and avenge me against my enemies, who have most grievously wronged me. I trust in your immense power to avenge me, to make the wrongs right, to protect me from all my enemies and let me fulfill my life's destiny.

O Most Holy Death, Empress of the Underworld, who rules over the mysterious and majestic night, I have dangerous adversaries who seek my destruction. They persecute me and plot against me by day and night; they disturb the peace of my mind and cause me great anxiety. I ask that you use the powers of your holy office to strike down my enemies, both great and small, by the power of your holy scythe. Let all who harass me, who pose a threat to me or my interests, be crushed beneath your feet. Let them nourish the soil and be food for the worms. I place all my trust in you, O Most Holy Death, my most powerful guardian and protector, because I know you will never forsake me!

Meditation of the Black Santa Muerte for the Release of Innocent Prisoners: *O Most Holy Death, Mother of All, I ask that you release N. from prison. Let the prison doors swing open and let him (or her) cross the threshold to total freedom.*

Creativity and Increased Mental Powers with the Blue Santa Muerte

Meditate with the blue Santa Muerte to obtain information about the physical world, for creative inspiration, wisdom, increased mental powers, and the ability to focus very intensely on your purpose. The blue Santa Muerte is especially good for writers, musicians, artists and other creative people, as well as students, researchers and journalists.

Meditation of the Blue Santa Muerte: *O Most Holy Death, I ask for your guidance and inspiration. Help me to keep a clear, calm, focused mind, so that I am unwavering in my purpose, even amidst chaos. Guide my hand, lead me to innovative ideas and creative solutions to problems. Send the muses to accompany me as I work, so that I may be at one with my own creative divinity.*

Peace and Harmony in the Home with the Bone-colored Santa Muerte

Meditate with the bone-colored Santa Muerte to bring domestic tranquility, harmony, and happiness to your home.

Meditation of the Bone-colored Santa Muerte: *O Most Holy Death, I ask that you enlighten my home with your holy presence and protect those who dwell here from all evil. Please, bless our home so that kindness, thoughtfulness, generosity, and a spirit of cooperation and sharing always prevail. Foster loyalty among us and let there always be peace, harmony, love, understanding, and gentleness. Bless us all with humility in our dealings with each other. Let us each consider the comfort, needs, and desires of others before those of ourselves.*

Spirit Communication, Divination, Finding Lost Objects, and the Protection of Pets with the Brown Santa Muerte

Santa Muerte guides the spirits of the dead to the Underworld and she knows each one. When asked, she will act as a go-between, facilitating communication between the living and the spirits of the dead. Brown is a less common color of Santa Muerte, which is used for spirit communication, divination, to locate lost objects and for the protection of family pets. In many cases, when she is invoked for such purposes, she communicates in dreams or gives her devotees flashes of insight.

Meditation of the Brown Santa Muerte for Spirit Communication and Divination: *O Most Holy Death, I ask that you calm my mind and sharpen my senses, so that I may easily send and receive communications from other worlds. When I ask questions, let me receive only true answers. Show me what I need to know to help myself and others.*

Meditation of the Brown Santa Muerte to Find Lost Objects: *O Most Holy Death, I have lost something dear to me. Please, help me find it right away.*

Meditation of the Brown Santa Muerte for the Protection of Pets: *O Most Holy Death, please, protect my beloved pet from all harm, accident, disease and malice. If he (or she) wanders, always return him (or her) to me safely.*

Exorcism with the Copper or Black Santa Muerte

The copper Santa Muerte and, because copper is a less commercially available color, sometimes the black Santa Muerte are employed to remove evil spirits from a place or to dissolve the attachment of evil spirits to people.

Meditation of the Copper or Black Santa Muerte for Exorcism: *O Most Holy Death, purge this place of all evil and drive all unwholesome spirits away by the power of your holy scythe. Fill this place with the power of your holy presence, expel the last trace of evil from this dwelling and break and destroy forever any and all negative spiritual attachments to those who reside here. Let there be peace and tranquility, now and forever more.*

Wealth and Success with the Gold Santa Muerte

The gold aspect of Santa Muerte is for abundance, attaining wealth, power, success, and good fortune. Santa Muerte has access to the treasures of the earth and power over all earthly affairs. You may ask her for exactly what you need, but you would be wise to ask for more; you will not be perceived as greedy if you ask for what you need to be comfortable. Santa Muerte will deliver without judgment. Furthermore, she will guard your accumulated wealth from those who wish to take it from you.

Meditation of the Gold Santa Muerte: *O Most Holy Death, Guardian and overseer of the treasures of the Earth, arrange it so I have all the money I need to meet all my financial obligations and live free of worry. Let me accumulate the abundant reserves I require for my financial comfort. Guard my prosperity from prying eyes. Dispel all evil influences and safeguard me from all envy surrounding my business and financial affairs. Destroy all my enemies, both great and small, who represent a threat to my business, career or financial* *well-being.*

Success in Court and Beneficial Contracts with the Green Santa Muerte

Meditate with the green Santa Muerte, which represents her ability to either balance or tip the scales of justice and to unite people's minds on a single idea, when you are faced with situations involving the court system and contracts.

Meditation of the Green Santa Muerte for Success in Court: *O Most Holy Death, allow me to obtain the outcome I seek in court. Influence the minds of the mortals who must judge my case so they see things my way.*

Meditation of the Green Santa Muerte for Guidance with Contracts: *O Most Holy Death, be my advocate and counsel, stay by my side and guide my hand. Let me only enter into agreements which are beneficial to me and my interests.*

High Spiritual States, the Removal of Obstacles, and Impossible Cases with the Purple Santa Muerte

The purple aspect of Santa Muerte is for achieving very high spiritual states, the acquisition of esoteric knowledge and occult power, and to remove all obstacles that stand in the way of attaining your personal goals. Santa Muerte is, also, a miracle worker who may be called upon in seemingly impossible cases.

Meditation of the Purple Santa Muerte to Achieve High Spiritual States and the Acquisition of Esoteric Knowledge and Occult Power: *O Most Holy Death, I am ready to experience the greatest blessings of your power. I am open to all you have to teach me. Fill me with the powers possessed by your wise owl companion; let me see that which is hidden in the darkness. Cast aside the veil of the spiritual world and attune my mind to the Akashic field, so that I may have knowledge of all things. Let the esoteric sciences be like an open book to me; give me the ability to discern the* *ways of the universe, so that I may know the creative forces and reap the benefits of this knowledge and power.*

Meditation of the Purple Santa Muerte to Remove Obstacles: *O Most Holy Death, allow me to view this situation from a higher perspective so I can easily see a clear path to my goals. If any obstacles block my way, destroy them by your mighty hand. Be my guide and benefactor, arrange circumstances to my advantage so I may easily obtain that which I desire.*

Meditation of the Purple Santa Muerte for Impossible Cases: *O Most Holy Death, I invoke you to ask for your assistance. That which is impossible to others is but a trifle for you. Your work is a miracle to some, but not to me, for I know your unlimited power and intelligence. I ask that you intervene on my behalf and bring your immense power to bear on this situation.*

Success in Love with the Red Santa Muerte

Meditate with the red Santa Muerte to bring love into your life and keep it. Santa Muerte wants loyal, loving relationships for her devotees and does not like to see her children in anguish. She is especially adept at bringing back lost or wandering lovers and stopping outside interference in your relationships.

Meditation of the Red Santa Muerte: *O Most Holy Death, I ask that you surround me with love that is loyal and true. Let nothing and no one come between my love and me and, if ever we must be apart, bring him (or her) back to me swiftly and safely. Let my true love's heart burn with love for only me, now and forever more.*

Good Fortune and Monetary Success with the Silver Santa Muerte

Silver, a less common color of Santa Muerte, is used for good fortune and financial success. You may, also, use this meditation with the gold Santa Muerte.

Meditation of the Silver Santa Muerte: *O Most Holy Death, I ask for your blessing upon my financial affairs. Let a steady flow of money come to me so that neither I nor anyone I care for lacks or is ever deprived of the things we need. Keep my pantry full and give me plenty to share with others. Let good fortune accompany me all the days of my life and bless me forever with your guiding presence.*

The Protection and Healing of Children and Peace in the Home with the White Santa Muerte and the Guardian Angel Santa Muerte

The white aspect of Santa Muerte is for the healing and protection of children and maintaining peace in the home. Traditionally, this color is associated with death in Mexico and young or unmarried people are buried dressed in white. Santa Muerte is sometimes depicted as a winged Guardian Angel with two children by her side. This image comes in a variety of colors and is primarily used for the protection of children and the family.

Meditation of the White Santa Muerte for the Protection and Healing of Children: *O Most Holy Death, bless this child, N., with good health and protect him (or her) from all evil, whether incarnate or discarnate. Wrap your loving arms around this child and nestle him (or her) in the comfort of your holy mantle.*

Meditation of the White Santa Muerte for Peace in the Home: See the *Meditation of the Bone-colored Santa Muerte* above.

Meditation of the Guardian Angel Santa Muerte: *O Most Holy Death, watch over my children and my loved ones, keep them safe from all harm. Let no accident befall them, fortify their bodies against all disease, and preserve them from all evil, envy and malice.*

Good Fortune and Increased Intellectual Powers with the Yellow Santa Muerte

The yellow aspect of Santa Muerte brings good fortune to all your endeavors, including contests and games of chance. It is, also, the aspect of Santa Muerte that is well-suited to philosophers, scientists and academics. It opens up a channel of wisdom to you and helps you to be successful in making right choices and drawing the right conclusions.

Meditation of the Yellow Santa Muerte: *O Most Holy Death, I ask you to turn the wheel of fortune in my favor. Bless me with your guidance and counsel, so that my endeavors succeed, so that my pursuits are generously rewarded and the work I do bears good fruit. Make me a channel for your infinite knowledge and wisdom, so that every move I make is always the right one.*

Guardianship, Comfort and Strength with the Santa Muerte Piadosa

The image of the Santa Muerte Piadosa (pronounced Pee-ah-doh-sah) is based on Michelangelo's famous sculpture, "Pieta," in St. Peter's Basilica in the Vatican in Rome, Italy. "Pieta" means both piety and pity. The Santa Muerte Piadosa holds a man and sometimes the skeleton of a man or a child in her arms and looks down upon him with tender mercy, representing the compassion of Santa Muerte and the fact that her devoted children are under her care.

When you are anxious, depressed or tired and weary and feel you cannot go another step, invoke the powers of mercy, compassion, and strength represented by the Santa Muerte Piadosa to carry you through.

Meditation of the Santa Muerte Piadosa: O Most *Holy Death, I ask for your strength and compassion. I am so weary from all my worries that I feel I cannot go on. I am overcome by my sorrows and I have fallen into despair. But, I know that because of your infinite love for me, your devoted child, you will lift my heavy burden. You will take from me all my troubles, dread, and despair and replace it with hope, happiness, and sweet relief. I now place myself and all my cares in your hands because I know that you will set things right.*

GEMSTONE CORRESPONDENCES TO
SANTA MUERTE'S POWERS

The specific aspects of Santa Muerte's power, which are reflected by the iconography and various colors found in the images of her, also have counterparts in the intrinsic mineral properties of gemstones. Gemstones are natural talismans because they store and radiate a particular type of energy depending on their mineral content. They may be used to forge a link between Santa Muerte's powers and the person who carries or wears them. They may, also, be used as accumulators and generators of her power to feed a particular kind of energy to the altar.

Choose polished or raw gemstones, or look for gemstones carved in the shape of skulls, owls or other images, such as the bat, wolf, or cat, which reflect her nocturnal spiritual nature. Select a shape that best represents your purpose.

Skulls represent the power of Most Holy Death. Their energy is that of Santa Muerte, herself. It is a good image to use for any aspect of her powers.

The owl's energy is that of the spiritual messenger of Most

Holy Death, able to see in the darkness, the owl is the possessor of occult knowledge. Owls bring communications to the living from the world of the dead, often warning of impending danger.

The bat's energy is that of concealment. Bats are, also, associated with fertility, birth, death, and good fortune.

The wolf's energy is that of fierce protection, including protection from evil spirits, misfortune, and disease.

The cat's energy is that of guardianship and good fortune. The black cat is one of Santa Muerte's common spiritual companions.

Wolves, owls, and cats all possess the spiritual energy of deadly, nocturnal predators and, therefore, may be useful in cases involving protection from dangerous enemies and revenge.

In the pages below, you will find a list of gemstones that correspond to aspects of Santa Muerte's power. The colors of the gemstones do not always match the colors of Santa Muerte because the correspondences are based on the mineral content of the stone and its intrinsic properties, rather than the stone's color. For instance, the emerald is a green stone, but when it is used for protection, it should be used with the Black or White Santa Muerte, both of which are for protection. Just as white Santa Muerte statues and talismans are regarded as neutral, clear quartz may be used for any purpose whenever specific gemstones cannot be found.

Examples

The following examples illustrate how you might choose an appropriate talisman and meditation for a particular purpose:

If you are suffering from anxiety and wish to be protected from the onset of anxiety attacks, choose an amethyst gemstone, perhaps carved into the shape of a cat, then use the meditation associated with the Amber Santa Muerte from the previous chapter. Include your own personal petition, speaking from the heart.

To improve your divination skills, choose a labradorite gemstone carved in the shape of an owl, then use the meditation of the Brown Santa Muerte for Spirit Communication and Divination, which may be found in the previous chapter.

For success in business, choose a citrine gemstone carved in the shape of a skull to represent all of Santa Muerte's powers or in the shape of a cat to represent good fortune, then use the meditation of the Gold or Silver Santa Muerte from the previous chapter.

To protect and conceal your personal possessions, choose a ruby in the shape of a bat, then use the meditation of the White or Black Santa Muerte, including your own petition.

For success in childbirth, choose an ammonite stone in its natural, raw state, which suggests the spiral of life, and use the meditations for the Amber Santa Muerte and the Santa Muerte with Child from the previous chapter.

Many powerful gemstones, which are ideal for your particular situation, may only be available in their raw form. This is perfectly fine. The above are only illustrative examples of how you might choose the right object and type of meditation for a particular purpose.

Let the information below, together with your own intuition, be your guide. The color aspect of Santa Muerte to use in meditation is indicated by the color and iconography associated with that particular office of her powers, which is listed after the words, "Santa Muerte Color," below. If you are ever in doubt about which color of Santa Muerte to use for a meditation or for any other purpose, you may, also, consult the *Appendix* for a quick list of her colors and correspondences.

Healing Adults

Santa Muerte Color: Amber and sometimes orange; use the Santa Muerte with Child for situations involving pregnancy

Gemstones:

Anxiety: Amethyst
Anxiety and depression: Ammonite
Bones and teeth: Howlite
Chakra balancing: Selenite
Cleansing and emotional balance: Orange calcite

Infections and general malaise: Amber
Insomnia: Howlite
Nervous conditions: Epidote
Pain: Garnet; blue sapphire
Pregnancy:
  Childbirth: Ammonite; picture jasper
  Conception, pregnancy and birth: Moonstone
  Protection from illnesses and birth defects: Apricot agate
  Protection from miscarriage: Chrysocolla
Protection from illness: Jade
P.T.S.D. and extreme anxiety: Richterite
Recovery from illness or trauma: Bloodstone; dragon blood jasper
Restoration of energy to the body, adrenal fatigue: Red jasper; boji stones
Thymus and throat: Angelite
Weight (Ideal): Amazonite; epidote; unakite

Breaking Addictions and Bad Habits

Santa Muerte Color: Amber

Gemstones:

Addiction, especially to alcohol: Amethyst; barite; blue sapphire
To break bad habits: Blue tiger's eye; dragon blood jasper; iolite

Healing Children

Santa Muerte Color: White and the Guardian Angel Santa Muerte

Older children may hold the item or wear it in a small pouch. For infants or very small children, place the item beneath the crib or bed, preferably near the head.

Gemstones: (Also, see those listed for adults.)

Distress: Amethyst; prehnite (phrenite)
Insomnia and nightmares: Chrysoprase

Protection of the Home

Santa Muerte Color: Black

Gemstones:

Protection from evil people and spirits: Black obsidian
Protection of possessions: Halite; quartz; ruby

Peace and Harmony in the Home

Santa Muerte Color: Bone-color or white

Gemstones:

Peace: Amethyst; aventurine; rose quartz
Strong family and loyalty: Emerald

Personal Protection

Santa Muerte Color: Black or white

Gemstones:

General protection: Angelite; selenite
Protection of possessions: Jaspers; ruby; sardonyx
Protection from black magic: Emerald
Protection from crime: Jaspers; sardonyx
Protection from envy and the Evil Eye: Black obsidian; black tourmaline; carnelian; jet; malachite; tiger's eye
Protection from evil spirits: Black tourmaline; black coral; hematite; malachite
Protection from illness and disease: Chalcopyrite; cavansite; jade; jaspers
Protection from injury: Turquoise
Protection from poison: Serpentine
Protection from police brutality: Jet
Protection from psychic attack: Amber; black kyanite; jade
Protection from psychic intrusion: Carnelian
Protection from robbery: Zircon
Protection from storms: Aquamarine; emerald (especially storms at sea)
Protection from violence: Jet
Protection from violent death: Amethyst
Protection during travel:
  Invisibility: Bloodstone
  Protection from theft during travel: Turquoise
  Travel by air: Malachite
  Travel by land: Amethyst; blue sapphire; garnet; turquoise
  Travel by water: Aquamarine; moonstone; pearl

Protection of Children

Santa Muerte Color: White and the Guardian Angel Santa Muerte

Gemstones:

General protection: Blue lace agate; green moss agate
Newborns: Mother of pearl
Protection from the Evil Eye: Jet (most commonly); malachite

Protection of Pets

Santa Muerte Color: Brown

Gemstones:

General protection: Black onyx; blue calcite; coral; fluorite; malachite; turquoise
Protection from illness and trauma: Carnelian
Reptiles: Black obsidian

Total Protection from Enemies: Hexing and Revenge

Santa Muerte Color: Black

Gemstones:

Hexing and cursing: Black obsidian; clear quartz; diamonds; jet; purple sapphire
Revenge: Emerald
To be forewarned of enemies: Blue sapphire
To defeat enemies: Coral; yellow sapphire

Exorcism: To Dispel Evil Spirits

Santa Muerte Color: Copper or black

Gemstones: Emerald; jet

Justice and Legal Matters

Santa Muerte Color: Green

Gemstones:

Beneficial contracts: Bloodstone
Marriage contracts: Pearl; peridot
Law Keep Away (Contra la Ley): Sardonyx
Legal justice:
  Compassion and courage: Jade
  Fairness: Malachite
  To prevail in court: Bloodstone
  To reveal truths and for victory: Emerald

To Free Prisoners

Santa Muerte Color: Black

Gemstone: Malachite

Money, Wealth, and Success

Santa Muerte Color: Gold or silver

Gemstones:

General success: Aventurine; citrine; green tourmaline; moss agate
Money: Green aventurine; citrine; malachite; pyrite; ruby
Success in business: Aventurine; citrine

Success in career: Aventurine; bloodstone; malachite
Wealth: Emerald; ruby

To Open Roads and Remove Obstacles

Santa Muerte Color: Purple

Gemstones: Blue kyanite; kunzite; red garnet; red spinel; red tourmaline; ruby; sapphire

Good Luck

Santa Muerte Color: Yellow

Gemstones:

Gambling: Aventurine
General good fortune: Jade
To make right decisions: Topaz
Victory: Emerald

Love and Romance

Santa Muerte Color: Red

Gemstones:

Love attraction: Emerald; rose quartz
Lover return: Moonstone
Passion: Rose quartz; ruby
Romance: Emerald; garnet; red coral; rose quartz; ruby
Reconciliation: Kunzite; rhodochrosite; rose quartz
To attract a good mate: Rhodonite
To curb sexual impulses: Emerald; onyx
To increase sexual desire: Carnelian

Spirit Communication, Divination, and E.S.P.

Santa Muerte Color: Brown

Gemstones:

Channeling and mediumship: Calcite; merlinite
Clairaudience and clairvoyance: Carnelian; merlinite; turquoise; Super Seven crystal (Sacred Seven stone or Melody's stone)
Clairvoyance: Iolite; sapphire; tiger's eye
Communication with the dead: Jade; prehnite
Communication with spirits in other realms: Azurite; celestite; fluorite; lapis lazuli; merlinite; sodalite; tanzanite; turquoise
Divination: Labradorite
Dowsing: Carnelian; brecciated jasper
E.S.P.: Black tourmaline; celestite; fluorite; lapis lazuli; obsidian; sapphire; tanzanite
Inspiration: Moonstone
Intuition: Amethyst; fluorite; moonstone
Precognition and prophesy: Labradorite; prehnite
Protection from psychic intrusion: Carnelian; chiastolite
Prophetic dreams: Ammonite; nebula stone
Psychometry: Carnelian
Scrying (crystal or mirror-gazing): Black obsidian
Telepathy: Amber; tiger's eye; ulexite

To Find Lost Objects

Santa Muerte Color: Brown

Gemstone:

Lost objects: Boulangerite; chalcopyrite; peridot; snakeskin agate
Lost objects, people, or pets: Unakite
Lost money or treasure: Green moss agate

Impossible Cases

Santa Muerte Color: Purple

Gemstone: Blue lace agate

Occult Powers and High Spiritual States

Santa Muerte Color: Purple

Gemstones:

Access to higher realms: Apophyllite; merlinite; moldavite; selenite
Angelic communication: Angelite; celestite; prehnite
Astral projection: Brecciated jasper; calcite; kyanite; red jasper; yellow jasper

Bilocation: Amethyst; barite; black obsidian; calcite; goethite; moqui balls (mochi marbles)
Higher states of consciousness: Moldavite
Invisibility: Bloodstone
Out-of-body experiences: Amethyst; black obsidian; calcite; goethite;
Telekinesis: Cacoxenite; Super Seven crystal; tunellite
Transmogrification: Barite; moqui balls; black obsidian
True perceptions or discernment: Unakite

Mental Focus and Creativity

Santa Muerte Color: Blue

Gemstones:

Acting and auditions: Red jasper
Artists: Iolite
Focus and meditation: Ametrine; blue aventurine; hematite; lapis lazuli; rainbow fluorite; sodalite; tanzanite; tourmaline
Creativity: Red aventurine; Botswana agate; carnelian; citrine; dolomite; garnet; orange calcite; peach aventurine; pyrite
Imagination: Aventurine
Mental Programming, to Break: Malachite; snowflake obsidian
   Ancestral and intergenerational programming: Petrified wood
   Emotional patterns: Aquamarine; blue kyanite; peridot
   Thought patterns: Amethyst; blue kyanite
Musicians: Rhodonite
Visualization: Iolite; green tourmaline
Will power: Alexandrite; blue tiger's eye; garnet; hematite; red jasper; prasiolite; sapphire; tiger iron
Writing and speaking: Angelite; barite; blue topaz; lapis lazuli; sodalite

Academics, Learning, and Wisdom

Santa Muerte Color: Yellow

Gemstones:

Academics: Coral calcite
Analysis: Sodalite; sphene (titanite)
Intellect: Apatite; pyrite; yellow fluorite
Knowledge: Peridot

Logic: Sodalite
Mathematics: Pyrite
Memory and achievement: Howlite; pink manganocalcite
Right conclusions: Blue tiger's eye; rainbow fluorite; topaz; tourmaline
Wisdom: Amber; fuchsite; jade; labradorite

The Accumulation and Direction of Gemstone Energy

As you work with these objects, they very naturally absorb the energy from your mind and body. The intrinsic energy of a gemstone is increasingly enhanced as you work with it and you forge an ever-stronger bond between the object, Santa Muerte's powers, and yourself. The energy may be used to strengthen your altar, to help yourself or someone else, or to enhance your own abilities, as you desire.

Direct the energy from the gemstone to yourself by holding it and seeing the energy flowing out of the object into your own body. If the work you have done with a gemstone is to help someone else, order the energy to release into the body of the person for whom it is intended whenever they touch it. If the energy is to be released from a gemstone into the altar, direct its energy there, then seal it in until you are ready to work with it, again.

In any of these cases, you may direct the energy by simply saying, "*In the name of Most Holy Death, release your energy into _____.*" Then, visualize the energy flowing steadily out of the object exactly where and how you want it to go.

Sophia diGregorio

THE INFLUENCE OF NUMEROLOGY ON THE ALTAR

You may use numerology to influence the energy harmonic of your altar. This is by no means a necessity when working with Santa Muerte, but simply another way to focus and direct the energy of your altar.

Choose a number appropriate to your purpose, as follows:

1. Protection, the power of the night, independence
2. Love, loyalty, justice
3. Family, children, pets, learning, divination, mental focus, communication, inspiration, the three elements (fire, air and water)
4. Stability, harmony, the four corners of the earth, the four elements (fire, air, water, and earth), the four winds, to command elemental powers of the earth
5. Earthly affairs, temporal matters, power, money, success, to destroy obstacles, the five elements (Akasha, fire, air, water and earth)
6. Marriage, contracts, legal matters

7. Good fortune, peace, safe travel, creative power, impossible cases, lost objects, esoteric knowledge

8. Marriage, contracts, legal matters, justice

9. Inspiration, learning, strong mental focus, wisdom

10. Money, wealth, success

11. Spirit communication, fertility, pregnancy, childbirth

12. Revenge, powerful spiritual aid in achieving your ends

13. Death, birth, exorcism, ancestors, rejuvenation, powerful healing

Incorporate the appropriate numbers on your altar in as many ways as you can think of, for instance, in the number of offerings such as flowers, herbs, candles, and gemstones. You may, also, time your operations to an hour of the day that corresponds with your intention. When you light incense for a ritual, pass it in a clockwise direction over the altar the number of times appropriate to your purpose.

To further intensify the power of numerological influence on your altar, use the geometric candle arrangements for each number as shown in the *Illustrations* on page 51. To use some of these arrangements safely, it is important to have an altar with a large enough surface to accommodate the number of candles, an image of Santa Muerte and your offerings. Take caution not to place candles too close to the edge of the altar, of course, and if you have long sleeves or long hair, take precautions so that you do not burn yourself while setting up your altar or during the course of a ritual.

Mini-candles and votive candles in glass holders are recommended in place of larger, taller candles if you are using more than three. The author has successfully used battery-powered candles (flameless candles or LED candles) on the altar in place of, and in combination with, wax candles. This is a logical alternative, not only for safety, but because of the nature of batteries and electricity, which is very similar to the fundamentally binary metaphysical energy the altar is designed to generate. Battery-powered candles of different colors may be purchased from many online and brick-and-mortar sellers of household goods.

Additionally, the different arrangements of candles on the altar, as shown in the *Illustrations*, produce geometric formations, which can be visualized three-dimensionally:

Triangular arrangements strengthen the resonance of the energy and speed action.

Rectangular formations stabilize and steady the energy.

Quincunx (like the "five" face of a pair of dice) arrangements anchor power to the altar.

Two wax candles placed on either side of Santa Muerte may be used to determine the outcome of an event, as discussed in *Chapter 7. Divination with Santa Muerte.*

When you repeatedly use this system of coordinating numbers with the purpose of your ritual, it creates and solidifies the connection, in your subconscious mind, between those numbers and your objective. The number is a code for those influences associated with it. The purpose of this is to reduce the amount of mental energy you required to perform the ritual successfully.

Illustrations

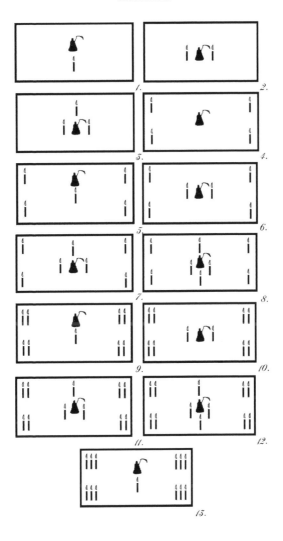

ALTAR ARRANGEMENTS FOR VARIOUS PURPOSES WITH PRAYERS

This chapter begins with a general discussion about Santa Muerte altars, including a reminder about the use of invocations, followed by descriptions of altar arrangements, which include the numerological suggestions from the previous chapter and accompanying prayers.

General Rules for Santa Muerte Altars

Make separate altars for different purposes. Altars, whether kept at home or at your place of business, should be placed discreetly in a common room or else in a separate room where they will not be seen and possibly derided by others, which can have a deleterious effect on their energy. Ideally, the altar should be oriented to the west (so that you are facing westward when you stand before it) because this is the direction of death, darkness, and the setting sun.

Keep a glass of clean, fresh water on the altar to facilitate the necessary environment for spirit communication. This helps to create the necessary atmospheric electrical charge. As a general rule, refresh offerings, at least, every three days and dust the altar once per week.

At least, one candle should be use in any arrangement. Candles are the primary offering to Santa Muerte. The wax may be seen as a representation of her earthly presence, the wick as representation of her spirit, and the flame as her divine power. The candle is a literal source of energy on the altar. The energy that is consumed in the burning of a candle is similar to the expenditure of electricity or any other kind of energy resource.

It is preferable to light candles with wooden matches. Their sulfur is both purifying and vivifying and the sound of the match being struck is a signal to your subconscious that the ritual has begun. When you do this regularly, your mind becomes conditioned to quickly shift into the proper frequency range and, in time, the trance state becomes automatic upon hearing the strike of the match.

During the course of a ritual, if you have the problem of a candle or candles repeatedly going out and not relighting and there is no physical explanation for this, such as a draft, discontinue your work. Generally, timing is not a problem for Santa Muerte, but it may be that there are other factors relevant to the situation that you are not yet aware of. Regroup, reconsider all the possibilities involved in the situation at hand, then choose another time to perform the ritual.

A Note Regarding the Use of Astrological Timing: While it is not necessary to wait until a particular day, hour, or phase of the moon to perform a ritual or spell successfully with Santa Muerte, the author has found that when the lunar phase and other aspects of astrological timing are right for the occasion, the results come remarkably quickly and large, seemingly impossible requests have been fulfilled overnight.

The most basic altar is comprised of the following items:

Black or purple image of Santa Muerte
Candles according to your purpose
Black or purple altar cloth
Glass of water
Offerings according to your purpose

It is sufficient to simply change the color of the candles on your altar to correspond with your purpose, however, you may completely tailor it. Customize your altar with hand sewn and embellished altar cloths and cloaks for Santa Muerte, especially if you have a knack for crafting. Nothing is automatically made better simply because it was assembled in a factory and when you put your personal energy into such things, it serves to strengthen the power of your altar.

Use containers made of crystal, glass, ceramic, iron or other metals. Avoid the use of plastic, Styrofoam, or paper plates and cups on the altar.

Before reciting any of the prayers in this book, invoke the elements and the spirit of Santa Muerte.

Invocations

The basis for common, contemporary styles of invocations to the elemental forces and to Santa Muerte are discussed in the first volume, *Grimoire of Santa Muerte: Spells and Rituals of Most Holy Death, the Unofficial Saint of Mexico.* Some of this information is mentioned, again, here as a reminder of its importance because it is through these invocations that you may easily call upon Santa Muerte and the natural forces that surround her.

There are two basic invocations that are used with prayers to Santa Muerte. The first is the *Invocation of the Spirit* or the elements, which summons the power of the creative force. The second is an Invocation to Santa Muerte, herself, which summons her spirit to you.

Reciting these invocations calls out to the elemental forces, which have a kind of intelligence of their own, and to the spirit of Santa Muerte. When they are used ritualistically, they help you to quickly focus your mind and prepare for the important work you are about to do.

Traditional Catholic-style Invocation of the Spirit

It is customary to begin and end all communications with Santa Muerte by reciting the *Our Father Prayer* and making the sign of the cross three times each as an *Invocation of the Spirit* or the elements. A Hermetic alternative to this is given in the *Grimoire of Santa Muerte: Spells and Rituals of Most Holy Death, the Unofficial Saint of Mexico.* Essentially, the purpose of this invocation is to initiate the flow of primal, elemental energy to the altar.

Our Father Prayer

Our Father,
Who art in heaven,
Hallowed be Thy name;
Thy kingdom come;
Thy will be done on earth as it is in heaven.
Give us this day our daily bread;
And forgive us our trespasses
As we forgive those who trespass against us;
And lead us not into temptation,
But deliver us from evil.

Make the sign of the cross as you say:

For thine (+) is the kingdom (+) and the power (+) and the glory (+) forever and ever. Amen.

Perform this three times as a means of invoking the elemental forces (the Tetragrammaton). Afterward, invoke Santa Muerte.

Catholic-style Invocation to Santa Muerte

O Lord, before your divine presence, the Holy Father, the Son and Holy Ghost, I ask permission to invoke Most Holy Death.

Pagan Invocation to Santa Muerte

By the powers of the earth, by the force of fire, by the inspiration of air, and the virtues of water, I invoke thee, Most Holy Death.

End your prayers by repeating the same *Invocation of the Spirit* you used at the beginning. Traditionally, recite the *Our Father Prayer* and cross yourself three times. These recitations at the beginning and end serve as a benediction and perform the function of priming and re-energizing the altar.

The following are altar arrangements for various purposes, with corresponding prayers to Santa Muerte:

Healing and Breaking Addictions

For healing and breaking addictions in adults, use the amber Santa Muerte and amber candles. Use orange for toxic or infectious conditions. For the healing of children, use white. The image of the Santa Muerte Incarnate may be used in any of these cases.

Amber, orange or white image of Santa Muerte or Santa Muerte Incarnate
Amber, orange or white candles
Amber, orange or white altar cloth
Photograph or personal effect
Aloe vera plant
Tobacco
Fresh fruit; for breaking addictions use lemons
Offerings in the number 13

Place a photograph or other personal effect of the person to be healed beneath the image of Santa Muerte.

Recite the following prayer:

O Most Holy Death, Powerful Queen of the Underworld,
Who walks between the worlds of the living and the dead,
I turn to you because I know your infinite power over the forces of life and death
And your promise to help all those in need who call upon you.
By your miraculous power, I ask that you heal this body.
I ask that you relieve all suffering from N., vanquish all illness, disease and pain.
Imbue his (or her) body with abundant life force energy,
Strengthen and invigorate his (or her) body and give him (or her) a strong will to live.
Surround him (or her) with your protection.
Let him (or her) now feel very healthy, be completely whole, and safe.
Break all negative habits and addictions that have taken hold of N.
Release all old patterns of negative emotions and negative thoughts.
Impart to him (or her) self-confidence and high self-esteem.
Let his (or her) desires only be for that which strengthens and revitalizes the body.
Destroy all negativity and replace it with joy, hope, and serenity.
O Most Holy Death, Great Mother of All, I believe and trust in you,
I ask that you always be a friend and guide to N., all the days of his (or her) life,
Always bless him (or her) with your guardianship.
[Insert your petition.]
O Most Holy Death, never leave my side, but be with me always, as my holy guardian,
In the name of the Father, the Son and the Holy Ghost. Amen.

For a Healthy Pregnancy and Safe Childbirth

Amber image of Santa Muerte or Santa Muerte with Child
Amber candles
Amber or white altar cloth
Copal or squaw vine
Corn, tortillas, or baked goods
Offerings in the number 11

Place a photograph or other personal effects of the woman to be protected beneath the image of Santa Muerte. If you perform this ritual for yourself, modify the wording as indicated in parentheses.

Recite the following prayer:

O Most Holy Death, who is Mother of All,
Wrap your holy mantle of protection around this woman (me),
Use your holy scythe to destroy all evil that attempts to go near her (me),
And provide her (me) with all the necessities of life.
Keep her (me) safe and healthy and let her (my) child be born in safety and health.
[Insert your petition.]
In the name of the Father, the Son and the Holy Ghost. Amen.

Protection

White image of Santa Muerte
White candle
White altar cloth
White roses or other flowers
Frankincense
Tequila, rum, or whiskey
Offerings in the number 1 for general protection or 12 for very strong protection.

Recite the following prayer:

O Most Holy Death, All-powerful Queen of the Underworld,
I ask that you enlighten my home with your holy presence
And embrace me in the serene comfort of your holy mantle.
O Most Holy Death, I implore you to be my shield and
My fiercest defender against all evil,
For there is no adversary you cannot overcome;
Even the most powerful and wicked must bend to your almighty will.
I ask that you use your immortal powers against all who seek to destroy me
Or to disturb the peace of my mind or my house.
Make my enemies, whether great or small, feel the blade of your holy scythe,
[Insert your petition.]
O Most Holy Death, never leave my side, even at times when I forget you,
Always be there, protecting me from the snares of my enemies.
In the name of the Father, the Son and the Holy Ghost. Amen.

Peace and Harmony in the Home

Bone-colored or white image of Santa Muerte
Ivory or white candles
Ivory or white altar cloth
White roses with the thorns removed
Incense
Angelica root
Candies, honey, and sweet breads
Offerings in the numbers 1, 3, or 4.
Recite the following prayer:

O Most Holy Death, Great Mother of All,
I ask that you enlighten my home with your holy presence
And illuminate it with the golden rays of your holy lamp.
By your infinite power and wisdom,
Bring peace and harmony to my home and all who dwell here.
Banish all discord, confusion, and conflict.
Grant us instead peace, understanding, empathy, and happiness.
[Insert your petition.]
Thank you for your loving kindness, and generosity, Most Holy Death.
Please, never forsake me all the days of my life, but always be by my side.

In the name of the Father, the Son and the Holy Ghost. Amen.

Blessing for a Child

Occasions which may call for the blessing of a child include birthdays, the beginning of a school year, or graduation.

White image of Santa Muerte or Guardian Angel Santa Muerte
White candles
White altar cloth
White roses
Tobacco
Copal
Fruits
Offerings in the numbers 1 or 3

Place a photograph or other personal effects of the child beneath the image of Santa Muerte.
Recite the following prayer:

O Most Holy Death, All-powerful Mother,
Who is the source from which all our blessings flow,
Who reigns on earth and in the Underworld,
Who is the special protector of the young and innocent,
Look favorably upon your child, N., and bless him (or her),
So that he (or she) shall grow ever stronger in wisdom and grace,
In happiness, with dignity and integrity.
Let him (or her) develop his (or her) individual gifts,
And spiritual, mental, and physical powers.
Let him (or her) succeed in all endeavors
With your protection and under your guidance.
Walk by his (or her) side and guide his (or her) steps,
As his (or her) guardian and generous benefactress,
Bless him (or her) in your name forever and ever.
O Most Holy Death, hear my prayer: [Insert your petition including the special blessings you desire for the child.]
In the name of the Father, the Son and the Holy Ghost. Amen.

Blessing for a Pet

Use this blessing ritual when you welcome a new pet into your home as a part of your family.

Brown image of Santa Muerte
Brown candles
Brown altar cloth
Tobacco
Copal
Tequila
Offerings in the numbers 1 or 3

Place a photograph of the pet beneath the image of Santa Muerte.

Recite the following prayer:

O Most Holy Death,
Please, bless and protect my beloved [name of your pet].
Let him (or her) have a happy life, free of disease and pain.
Keep him (or her) safe from all harm.
If he (or she) is ever lost, quickly return him (or her) to me.
In the name of the Father, the Son and the Holy Ghost. Amen.

Ritual for the Dying

At the time of death, a person sees a lifetime of events in review. The nature of these events determine the soul's next destination. The Catholic *Hail Mary* (sometimes called *Ave Maria*) prayer addresses this idea, which is far more ancient than Christianity and found throughout the world. You may use the prayer provided with this ritual in conjunction with the *Hail Mary* prayer to request Santa Muerte's absolution and mercy upon the dying:

Use white on the altar for infants, children, and the unmarried; use black for other people. Santa Muerte Piadosa or the Guardian

Angel Santa Muerte may be used in any case.

White or black image, Santa Muerte Piadosa, or Guardian Angel
Santa Muerte
White or black candles
White or black altar cloth
Tobacco
Copal
Tequila
Roses
Offerings in the number 13.

Place a photograph or other personal effects of the person
beneath the image of Santa Muerte.
Recite the following prayer:

O Most Holy Death, Empress of the Underworld,
Merciful Mother of All, who holds the scales of justice,
I ask that you purify the soul of N.,
And purge the Akashic records of his (or her) worldly transgressions.
Grant him (or her) all absolution and mercy.
O Most Holy Mother, Powerful Guardian and Guide,
Conduct his (or her) soul to the proper place,
And comfort and assuage the grief of the living
By the knowledge that his (or her) spirit is never far away.
[Insert your petition.]
O Most Holy Death, never forsake us all the days of our lives,
But be our loving guide, now and forever more.
In the name of the Father, the Son and the Holy Ghost. Amen.

Hail Mary Prayer

Hail Mary, full of grace,
The Lord is with thee;
Blessed art thou amongst women,
And blessed is the fruit of thy womb, Jesus.
Holy Mary, Mother of God,

Pray for us sinners,
Now and at the hour of our death. Amen.

Total Protection from Dangerous Enemies: Hexing and Revenge

Black image of Santa Muerte
Black candles
Black altar cloth
Black roses, artificial or dyed
Tequila
Tobacco
Valerian root
Offerings in the numbers 1 or 12

If the name of your enemy is known to you, write it on the petition paper; if it is unknown, simply write the words, "*My enemy.*" Precisely describe the nature of your problem and what outcome you desire in your petition.

Recite the following prayer:

O Most Holy Death, Almighty Queen of the Night,
My most powerful protector and benefactor,
I ask for your protection from a dangerous adversary.
He gives me no peace, day and night, he plots against me,
He slanders my good name and threatens me at every turn,
and, because of him, I fear for my safety and my very life.
Therefore, I ask that you, by the power of your holy office,
Turn his own devious machinations, plots, and devices upon him.
If my enemy advances toward me, drive him back.
If he makes a move against me, strike him down.
If he tries to come near me, cut him off, destroy him,
Grind his bones to dust, and lay his body to waste.
O Most Holy Death, I trust in you because I know your power.
I confide in you because I know you will defend me to the death against this formidable foe.
[Insert your petition.]

I know that you will never forsake me, that you will let no harm come to me.

I ask that you always remain by my side and be my holy protector all the days of my life.

In the name of the Father, the Son and the Holy Ghost. Amen.

Exorcism: To Dispel Evil Spirits

Copper or black image of Santa Muerte
Copper or black candles
Black altar cloth
Holy Water
Basil or white sage (Salvia apiana)
Fruits and vegetables, especially lemons and lettuce
Offerings in the number 13

Recite the following prayer:

O Most Holy Death, Almighty Queen of the Night,
Who knows all the spirits on earth and in the netherworld,
Who commands legions of demons and armies of angels,
I ask that you enlighten this place with your holy presence
And fill the hearts of those who dwell here with peace and love.
O Most Holy Death, Empress of the Underworld,
I ask that you use the infinite powers of your holy office to cast out
All unwholesome, unwanted, and wicked spirits from this place.
Wield your holy scythe to sever all their connections
To this place and to all who dwell here, forever and ever.
Cleanse and forever render this place free of these spirits.
[Insert your petition.]
In the name of the Father, the Son and the Holy Ghost. Amen.

When you have completed this prayer, sprinkle Holy Water in each room and corridor of the house while making the sign of the cross and repeating an Invocation to Santa Muerte.

Justice, Contracts, and Other Legal Matters

Green image of Santa Muerte
Green candle
Green altar cloth
Cigars or cigarettes
1 to 4 apples, halved and drizzled with honey
Offerings in the numbers 2, 6, or 8

Place a copy of the contract or documents related to the case beneath the image of Santa Muerte.

Recite the following prayer:

O Most Holy Death, Almighty Queen of the Underworld,
My most powerful advocate and only judge, who has power over all earthly affairs,
I ask you to arrange it so that I only enter into agreements that are beneficial to me.
Let it be that I always receive leniency and mercy in all legal matters and court cases.
[Insert your petition.]
O Most Holy Death, always be by my side as my wise counsel,
Guide me every step of the way and never forsake me all the days of my life.
In the name of the Father, the Son and the Holy Ghost. Amen.

For the Release of a Prisoner

Use the following altar arrangement and prayer for the release of a prisoner. If the person is innocent, you need not do anything more, however, if the person is guilty, he or she must promise to make full restitution to the injured party, to make a sacrifice of something to the honor of Santa Muerte (such as quitting a vice), and make a solemn vow never to commit such an act ever, again.

Black image of Santa Muerte
Black candles
Black altar cloth
Holy Water
Tequila
Cigars
Old key(s) on a ring, iron is preferred
Carnations
Offerings in the numbers 1 or 12

Place a photograph or other personal effects of the prisoner beneath the image of Santa Muerte.
Recite the following prayer:

O Most Holy Death, Almighty Queen of the Underworld,
Who holds the keys to open all doors,
And who is a friend to all who have been treated unfairly in life,
I come to you because I know your great power and compassion.
I know that there is nothing that you cannot do.
I ask that you unlock the prison door and let it swing open,
So that N, may walk through it to freedom.
O Most Holy Death, whose powers on earth and in the netherworld are infinite,
Please, free N. and give him (or her) a second chance at life.
[Insert your petition.]
In the name of the Father, the Son and the Holy Ghost. Amen.

Prosperity

Gold image of Santa Muerte
Gold candles
Gold altar cloth
Golden yellow flowers
Rue, basil, or wormwood
Small bowl of corn, wheat, rice, or other grains
Coins of different denominations
Bread, tortillas, or other baked goods
Offerings in the numbers 5 or 10.

Recite the following prayer:

O Most Holy Death, Empress of the Underworld,
My most generous and trusted benefactor,
Who governs the treasures of the earth,
Who wields the holy scythe of the harvest,
Who holds the scales of justice,
Who is the clearest, brightest light in the darkness,
I ask you to use the powers of your holy office,
To intervene in worldly affairs on my behalf.
By virtue of your dominance in the Underworld
And your rulership of the treasures of the earth,
Which are infinitely abundant,
Please, grant me riches and good fortune.
Let abundant wealth flow freely to me,
Lavish me in the abundance of your infinite love,
Let my life be easy and worry free,
And let no one under my roof ever lack what they need.
[Insert your petition.]
O Most Holy Death, I am grateful for your compassion and generosity,
Never leave my side, but be my holy guide and guardian, now and forever more,
In the name of the Father, the Son and the Holy Ghost. Amen.

Good Fortune and Success in Business, Sales, and Career

Gold, yellow, or white image of Santa Muerte
Gold, yellow, or white candles
Gold, yellow, or white altar cloth
White or yellow roses
White plate
Glass of red wine
Cigars or cigarettes
Ashtray (optional)
Gold, silver, or copper coins
Assorted hard candies
Offerings in the number 5

Arrange the coins and candies on a gold, yellow, or white plate and set it before the image of Santa Muerte. Arrange the glass of wine next to the plate and the ashtray and the roses beside her image. If you smoke, smoke one of the cigars or cigarettes and place the others in the ashtray.

Recite the following prayer:

O Most Holy Death, My Most Powerful Benefactor,
Who holds power over earthly affairs,
And whose wisdom and compassion are infinite,
I ask that you enlighten this place with your holy presence.
Turn the wheel of fortune in my favor
And by your earthly powers arrange my affairs so that
Prosperity and abundance continually flows through these doors.
I know your love and concern for the welfare of your beloved children.
Grant me your guidance and infinite wisdom,
So that every decision I make is the right one.
Grant me success in all my endeavors and raise me up in life.
When I sow a seed, let it multiply by one thousand,
So that I prosper and continue to prosper until I become exceedingly wealthy.
[Insert your petition.]
O Most Holy Death, thank you for providing me with all I need.

Never leave my side, but be my holy guide and guardian, now and forever more,
In the name of the Father, the Son and the Holy Ghost. Amen.

To Destroy Obstacles

Purple image of Santa Muerte
Purple candles
Purple altar cloth
Coffee
Sea Salt
Chicory
Offerings in the number 5

Recite the following prayer:

O Most Holy Death, Almighty Queen of the Underworld,
Whose powers on earth and in the netherworld are infinite,
I know that what is a miracle to some is but a trifle to you.
I am faced with difficulties beyond my control,
Which stand as a boulder in my path.
I ask that, by the power of your holy scythe,
You destroy all such obstacles and clear the way for me to go forward.
[Insert your petition.]
O Most Holy Death, I trust in you above all others.
Please, do not forsake me and never leave my side all the days of my life.
In the name of the Father, the Son and the Holy Ghost. Amen.

Good Luck and Success at Gambling

Perform this ritual before gambling. Use yellow in matters where studying information or developing your skill may improve your chances of winning. Use gold or silver, when it is a matter of pure chance.

Yellow, gold, or silver image of Santa Muerte
Yellow, gold, or silver candles
Yellow, gold, or silver altar cloth
Golden yellow flowers
Gold or silver coins
Old keys
Rue
Corn tortillas, corn, baked goods, or yellow apples
Offerings in the number 7

Recite the following prayer:

O Most Holy Death, My Most Generous Benefactor,
I ask that you send your holy messenger the owl
To come and whisper in my ear, so that I always know the right answer.
Shine your guiding light on my path,
So that every step I take is sure and steady.
Turn the wheel of fortune in my favor, so that I always succeed.
[Insert your petition.]
O Most Holy Death, stay by my side and never forsake me all the days of my life.
In the name of the Father, the Son and the Holy Ghost. Amen.

Love and Romantic Relationships

Perform this ritual to encourage love and loyalty in an existing romantic relationship between a couple.

Red image of Santa Muerte
Red candles
Red altar cloth
Red, pink, or white roses
Apples, halved, drizzled with honey, and sprinkled with powdered cinnamon and sugar
Plate upon which to place the apples
Rosemary
Chocolates
Dish of cinnamon candies
Offerings in the number 2; or in the numbers 6 or 8, if a legal marriage is part of the situation.

Place an image of the couple concerned or personal effects from each beneath the image of Santa Muerte.
Recite the following prayer:

O Most Holy Death, Most Powerful Mother of All,
Whose love for her children is infinite,
I ask that you enlighten our home with your holy presence,
Let there always be loyalty between me and my partner,
Let promises that are made be kept,
Let passion always be accompanied by compassion,
Empathy, understanding and kindness.
I especially ask that you [Insert your petition],
O Most Holy Death, grant us happiness, love, and peace,
And always be our loving guide and counselor all the days of our lives.
In the name of the Father, the Son and the Holy Ghost. Amen.

To Find Lost Objects

Brown image of Santa Muerte
Brown candles
Brown altar cloth
Sage (salvia officinalis)
Corn or corn tortillas
Old keys
Offerings in the number 7

Recite the following prayer:

O Most Holy Death, Powerful Queen of the Night
Who sees all and knows all,
By the power of your holy companion the owl,
Who calls to me in the darkness and whispers in my ear,
And your holy lamp, which is my guiding light in the night,
Grant me the ability to see that which is lost or hidden.
[Insert your petition.]
In the name of the Father, the Son and the Holy Ghost. Amen.

Impossible Cases

Purple image of Santa Muerte
Purple candle
Purple altar cloth
Tequila or whiskey
Rue
Photographs, documents, or personal effects
Offerings in the number 7

You may use fresh rue as an offering on the altar or burn dried rue as an incense. Place any documents, photographs, or personal effects related to your problem beneath the image of Santa Muerte.
Recite the following prayer:

O Most Holy Death, Almighty Queen of the Underworld
Whose powers on earth and in the world beyond are infinite,
I am faced with a desperate situation, which seems hopeless to me,
But, I know that nothing is impossible to you.
I know your love and compassion for your children,
So, it is to you I come with this request.
[Insert your petition.]
Please, arrange the circumstances surrounding these affairs in my favor.
In the name of the Father, the Son and the Holy Ghost. Amen.

Academic Success, Intellectual Pursuits, and Learning

This altar is especially good for scientists, researchers, teachers, counselors, and students.

Yellow image of Santa Muerte
Yellow candles
Yellow altar cloth
Yellow flowers
2 Lodestones
New sewing needles
Coffee
Rosemary, dried and crushed
Fresh fruit, vegetables, bread or other baked goods
Old keys
Offerings in the numbers 3 or 9

Write your name and other pertinent details on a piece of plain white paper, fold it twice and place it beneath the image of Santa Muerte. Place the lodestones on the altar and apply the needles to them.

Recite the following prayer:

O Most Holy Death, Almighty Queen of the Underworld,
Whose power and knowledge are infinite,
I ask that you teach me the truth about all things.
By the wisdom of your holy companion the owl,
Unlock the door to enlightenment and understanding
And set me on the path of illumination.
Grant me the ability to see that which others cannot or dare not.
Reveal to me the facts of any and all circumstances
And bless me with courage and the power of discernment.
I especially ask that you [Insert your petition].
O Most Holy Death, guide me now and always,
In the name of the Father, the Son and the Holy Ghost. Amen.

For Mental Focus and Creativity

This altar is especially good for writers, musicians, artists, researchers, journalists, and students.

Blue image of Santa Muerte
Blue candles
Blue altar cloth
Coffee
Violets
Old keys
Fresh fruit, vegetables, bread, or other baked goods
Offerings in the numbers 3, 7, or 9

Place fresh violets on the altar; dried, crushed violets may be incinerated.

Recite the following prayer:

O Most Holy Death, Almighty Queen of the Underworld,
Whose power and knowledge are infinite,
I ask that you free me from all worries and anxiety,
Calm my mind and steady my hand,
Sharpen my mental powers and increase my concentration,
Inspire and guide me.
Let me be a channel for your immense power.
[Insert your petition.]
O Most Holy Death, always stay by my side
And never forsake me all the days of my life.
In the name of the Father, the Son and the Holy Ghost. Amen.

Psychic Development and Divination Skills

This altar is especially good for psychics and mediums and those who wish to develop their divination skills. Old keys are placed on the altar in rituals that pertain to unlocking doors to information and other worlds. Old iron skeleton keys on a ring are the best choice. They may be found at antique stores.

Brown image of Santa Muerte
Brown candles
Brown altar cloth
Roses or carnations
Amber resin
Tobacco
Tequila
Old keys
Offerings in the number 3

Recite the following prayer:

O Most Holy Death, Almighty Queen of the Underworld
Whose powers on earth and in the kingdoms beyond are infinite,
I ask that you guide me on the path of psychic development.
Let me see and hear what is beyond the earthly realm.
Sharpen my senses to receive the finest vibrations,

Attune my mind to the rarified energy of the Akashic field.
Grant me the powers to know the past, present and future.
Turn the key and open the door for me to explore the metaphysical world.
[Insert your petition.]
In the name of the Father, the Son and the Holy Ghost. Amen.

Communication with Powerful Spirits

Use this altar arrangement to prepare for communication with spirits, including ancestors and any who may provide you with assistance or information.

Purple image of Santa Muerte
Purple candles
Purple altar cloth
Purple flowers
Copal resin
Chocolate
Tobacco
Tequila
Old keys
Offerings in the number 11

Recite the following prayer:

O Most Holy Death, Almighty Queen of the Underworld,
Who has the power to freely walk between worlds,
I ask that you empower me with the ability
To see, hear, feel, and speak with spirits,
Whether they be my ancestors or great and powerful minds,
Whether they have lived before in the flesh
Or whether they have always been discarnate.
Prepare me for this endeavor in every possible way.
Assist and expedite these communications.
Let me be a medium and a channel for your miraculous powers.
Open the way for me to explore the world of spirits.
[Insert your petition.]

O Most Holy Death, turn the key and open the door!
In the name of the Father, the Son and the Holy Ghost. Amen.

Note: These last three altar arrangements for the blue, brown and purple aspects of Santa Muerte are discussed in *Chapter 6. Three Rituals to Communicate with the Dead.* Instructions for a 3-day ritual are provided along with alternative prayers for the purpose of achieving a high level of mental focus, psychic ability, and mediumship.

PART 2.

THE OCCULT POWERS OF SANTA MUERTE

Sophia diGregorio

THREE RITUALS TO COMMUNICATE WITH THE DEAD

One of Santa Muerte's many important offices is to guide the souls of the dead through the Underworld, therefore, she knows every spirit and can easily locate them. She has the power to walk between the worlds of the living and the dead and is an intermediary between the two.

In the context of a séance, she performs the function of a control. If you ask Santa Muerte to let you speak with the spirits of those who have passed on, she will bring them to you quickly and reliably. Doing spiritualist work with the aid of Santa Muerte is very safe because she will protect you from any intrusions from unwholesome spirits who might, for example, pose as another spirit to deceive you or overstay their welcome.

Santa Muerte will, also, help to prepare you for this experience by increasing your ability to concentrate and expanding your natural psychic abilities. She will help you to banish any fears, whether conscious or subconscious, that might prevent you from effectively communicating with the spirits of the dead.

Preparation

To achieve success with your first session with Santa Muerte as an intermediary between the worlds of the living and the dead, conduct each of the rituals in this chapter over the course of three consecutive nights. The nature of each of the three nightly rituals is characterized by the colors, blue on the first night, brown on the second night, and ending with purple on the third night. Think of the final night as your appointment with the spirits of the dead.

The altar arrangements for these three candle colors are provided at the end of the previous chapter. You may use the basic altar of Santa Muerte for all three nights. For each night, set the altar according to its color and purpose.

On each of these nights, write a petition to Santa Muerte making specific requests regarding any spiritual goals you are trying to achieve. Before each session, light the candle(s), then place your hands on the altar and make your usual invocations before reciting the prayer. On the third night, you will be fully prepared to contact the spirits of the dead.

The First Night: Ritual of the Blue Candle

Superstition surrounds the subject of spirit communication, especially in Western culture, and fears associated with it may be so deeply embedded in your subconscious mind that you are not even aware of them. This can include a fear of being different, as well, because communicating with the dead is not especially common or accepted. It is important to release any fear in order to fully develop your natural psychic abilities.

The purpose of the ritual of this night is to obtain from Santa Muerte the blessing of greater wisdom and understanding of how communication with the dead works. It is, also, to help you establish a calm, steady focus, which will lead to greater sensitivity to subtle energetic vibrations.

Communication with the dead has an occult scientific explanation: Thoughts and images may be transferred from one mind to another, whether the parties are living or dead. Signals are transmitted from the mental body through the etheric field, much like a radio signal. Once received, they are processed by the mental body of the recipient. While the physical body may die, the mental body and other spiritual vehicles of the soul live on, retaining the same personality, memories, and knowledge that the person acquired in life.

Use the altar arrangement for the blue candle found at the end of the previous chapter. Make your usual invocations, then recite the following prayer to Santa Muerte:

O Most Holy Death, Almighty Queen of the Underworld,
Whose power and knowledge are infinite,
I ask that you free me from all worries and anxiety,
Calm my mind and steady my hand,
Sharpen my mental powers and increase my concentration,
Give me the calm, single-minded focus I need to transmit and receive spirit communications.
Strengthen my natural abilities, fine tune my senses, and expand my awareness.
Banish all fear and superstition from me and give me instead understanding and wisdom.
[Insert your petition.]
O Most Holy Death, I trust in you and I know you will let no harm come to me.
In the name of the Father, the Son and the Holy Ghost. Amen.

Benediction:

Conclude by invoking the spirit (the elements) three times.

Allow the candle to burn down completely while you remain in a quiet, calm state for the rest of the evening. Feel the presence of Santa Muerte around you.

The Second Night: Ritual of the Brown Candle

The purpose of this night's ritual is to awaken and expand your extra sensory perception, so that you are better able to send and receive information from the metaphysical world. With this ability, you can discern the true nature of the universe, gain esoteric knowledge, and explore other realms, including the Akashic field, which holds information about all things past, present and future.

Use the altar arrangement for the brown candle found at the end of the previous chapter. Make your usual invocations, then recite the following prayer to Santa Muerte:

O Most Holy Death, Almighty Queen of the Underworld,
Whose powers on earth and in the kingdoms beyond are infinite,
I ask that you attune my mind to the rarefied Akashic field,
Sharpen my senses to receive even the finest vibrations,
And give me knowledge of what lies in the past, present and future.
Let nothing be hidden from me,
But shine the light of your holy lamp on all of creation,
And reveal the ancient mysteries to me.
Infuse my body with an abundance of essential life force

And fill this place with the power of your holy presence.
[Insert your petition.]
O Most Holy Death, turn the key and open the door!
In the name of the Father, the Son and the Holy Ghost. Amen.

After you have recited the benediction, just as you did in the previous night's ritual, allow the candle to burn down while you remain in a meditative state, focused on the requests you have made to Santa Muerte. Allow your senses to grow sharper. Be aware of every sound, every motion, every sensation, however subtle. Experience the room you are in with these newly heightened senses. Then, from the place where you sit, use your expanded senses to explore the rest of your home and the area outside.

If you wish to perform a tarot or rune reading, use your pendulum, or perform any act of divination described in the proceeding chapters, it is a good time to do so. This ritual prepares you for accurate divination on this night and anytime in the future. It may be repeated anytime to boost your psychic powers.

The Third Night: Ritual of the Purple Candle

Purple is associated with the causal forces of the universe, those forces that set the creation of the universe in motion. It is the color of high spiritual states, psychic manifestations, and a high level of spirit communication, by which you can obtain powerful spiritual assistance.

This aspect of Santa Muerte relates to her primordial nature, which is the origin of her infinite power. It embodies the power of transformation as well as power over the spiritual and physical worlds. In short, all of the powers traditionally associated with witchcraft are epitomized by Santa Muerte's purple aspect.

To prepare for this night's ritual, clean your house and make it look neat and tidy, just as you would if you were expecting corporeal company. If you are contacting the spirit of someone you know, place items on the altar associated with him or her, including photographs, mementos, jewelry, or other items belonging to the person. Set a table and provide refreshments, exactly as if you were expecting physical guests. Partake of the refreshments at the end of the session.

If you are comfortable using a spirit (Ouija™) board, automatic writing planchette, or performing automatic writing with just a pen, prepare the items you need and place them on the same table where you plan to receive your guests. You may, also, set up a digital camera or record the session using a cassette or digital recorder.

Write a petition to Santa Muerte that includes the name of the spirit with whom you wish to speak. For example, write: "*O Most Holy Death, please, bring N. to me.*"

If you do not have the name of a spirit you wish to contact, but would like to speak with one who has a particular area of knowledge, write your request to that effect. If you are a writer or an artist, you may ask the spirits of deceased authors or artists to assist you with your work. If your interest is in science, or medicine, ask to communicate with spirits who are knowledgeable about these subjects. For example, write: "*Please, bring a knowledgeable physicist to me."*

Use the altar arrangement for the purple candle found at the end of the previous chapter. Repeat the same invocations as on the previous night, then recite the following prayer to Santa Muerte:

O Most Holy Death, Almighty Queen of the Underworld
Who has the power to freely walk between worlds,
Let me be a vessel for your miraculous power.
I ask that you use the authority of your holy office
To open the door to the spirit world tonight,
So that the spirits of the dead may come through.
Please, assist and expedite these communications at this time.
I, also, ask that you send good spirits and familiars to aid me.
[Insert your petition.]
O Most Holy Death, turn the key and open the door!
I am ready to receive my guest(s).
In the name of the Father, the Son and the Holy Ghost. Amen.

After you have completed this prayer, take your seat and wait in silence for a few minutes. If you do not receive a transmission right away, summon the spirit by saying: *By the power of Most Holy Death, I ask to speak to N. Then, continue to wait quietly and patiently.*

Often, if a particular spirit is unavailable, another spirit who is associated with him or her will come to speak to you. Sometimes someone appears, but you are not able to perceive their presence. So, even if it seems no one has come, after the session, review your camera footage or your audio recording. Santa Muerte may send spirits to communicate with you in real time, either mentally or through some physical manifestation, or they may come to you in a dream later that night.

Once contact is established and your first conversation takes place, you may make a request to the spirit to return to speak to you, again, at a designated time. Regularly holding such sessions and communicating with the same spirits helps to establish rapport and trust.

If your first session is not all you hoped for, do not be discouraged. Not everyone is the same with regard to how they communicate with the dead. Your mediumship and other psychic abilities are uniquely your own. If you are not yet familiar with your own particular talents, by holding sessions regularly, you will begin to discover them.

Regardless of how successful you feel your communication has been, thank the spirits for coming to speak with you. Then, return to your altar and recite the following prayer to Santa Muerte:

O Most Holy Death, thank you for presiding over this gathering and for sending the spirits to speak with me and returning them safely home. I ask that you now close the gate between the worlds until our next session.

Recite your benediction, as usual.

From this point forward, whenever you wish to speak with the spirits of the dead, perform this third night's ritual of the purple candle.

DIVINATION WITH SANTA MUERTE

Santa Muerte may be consulted as an oracle whenever you require information about the past, present, or future. She speaks to her devotees through dreams and by means of signs and symbols, however, she will assist you with any form of divination upon request.

One method of divination with Santa Muerte involves observing events on the altar, whenever you perform a ritual or spell. Performing such divination helps you to determine the efficacy of your work, to determine if more work must be done, to discover factors you may not have considered before, and to determine if the work needs to be taken in a different direction to be the most successful.

This chapter includes a guide to divination by means of both signs and symbols. Signs are events on the altar brought about by the movement of the energy there. Examples of such events include the behavior of a burning candle's flame, the way it drips, if it smokes, and the appearance of other offerings at the end of a working. Symbols are formed by energetic vibrations. Your interpretation of these manifestations is not entirely reliant on this guide, but on your own intuition and experience, as well.

Divination by Observing Candles

If you are working with one candle or a main candle on the altar, which is placed in front of the image of Santa Muerte, let it represent the situation at hand. If it is a taper or figure candle, inscribe your question on the side of it, otherwise, write the question on a piece of paper and place it beneath the candleholder.

If you have one candle on either side of the image of Santa Muerte, let the candle at her left hand represent the past and the candle at her right hand represent the future.

Candle Flames

Whenever you perform divination by observing candle flames, do so with the lights out or very dimmed. Sit very still in a room where there is no motion or draft. If you plan to read the wax drippings, do not use dripless candles. Trim candle wicks to 1/8" to 1/4" (3 to 6 mm) before lighting them. Allow the candle to burn, at least, 15 minutes before beginning your divination.

If the flame slowly rises and lowers repeatedly: The subject of your ritual is aware that you are doing this work.

If the flame is erratic or dances: Confusion; lack of calm focus.

If the flame remains static: Smooth, steady progress.

If it is a high flame: A powerful working; quick results.

If it is a small flame: Low energy; slow progress.

If the candle produces a twin flame: Another person is involved in the situation; an unseen force may be working against you.

If the flame sizzles, pops, or hisses: Spirits are trying to get your attention.

If the flame flickers: Reconsider your approach.

If the flame gives off sparks: Resistance; friction.

If the tip of the flame is very bright: Good fortune; success.

If the flame rotates clockwise: Success is certain.

If the flame rotates counterclockwise: Reversals; disappointment.

If the flame spirals: Expect good news.

Blue flame: Success

Red flame: Powerful, fast results.

White flame: Assistance is being rendered to you from the spirit world.

Yellow flame: Some difficulties; proceed with caution.

If the flame goes out or a candle will not relight: Your work is frustrated. Change your approach and try, again, at another time.

If an extinguished flame relights itself: The working is not complete. There is more to be done.

Candle Wax Drippings

If wax forms in drops on the side of the candle: Sorrow.

If two such forms appear on the side of the candle: Conflict; reconsider your point of view.

If wax drops form on the right side of the candle: Quick progress.

If wax drops form on the left side of the candle: Slow progress.

If there are many droplets: Sorrow; slow progress.

Other Signs

If the wick appears knotted: An especially complex situation.

If the candle burns down quickly: Quick results.

If the candle burns down slowly: Slow results.

If the candle fails to burn down entirely: The working was not completely thorough. There may be an issue you failed to address.

If the candle smokes: Strong adversity; powerful forces are working against you.

If the candle burns without smoking: Results will follow in due time; all will go smoothly.

If the glass encasing of the candle cracks or breaks: Resistance; yet unforeseen complications. While doing work against enemies, this is a sign that your adversary has strong spiritual protection.

If the glass is entirely black at the end of a working: Someone is working against you; psychic attack; or the Evil Eye.

If the candleholder is black at the top only: Negative energy directed toward you has been cleansed or dispelled.

If the glass is black at the bottom only: Obstacles remain.

If one side of the candleholder is scorched: Consider alternative solutions.

If flowers placed on the altar become shriveled and dry before three days: Great energy has been drawn from your offerings and you will see results very quickly.

If flowers shed petals upon the altar: Sorrow and grief.

To Receive an Answer to a Yes-no Question

To receive Santa Muerte's answer to a yes-no question, place two brown candles on the altar, one at her right hand and one at her left. Then, ask your question and light the candles. If the flame of the candle at her right hand goes out first, then the answer is "Yes." If the flame of the candle at her left hand goes out first, the answer is "No." If a candle's flame goes out soon after it is lit, do not relight it; this candle represents the answer to your question.

To Receive the Answer to a Multiple Choice Question

To ask Santa Muerte to give you the answer to a question that involves multiple possibilities, set aside a brown candle for each possible answer. On the side of each one, inscribe a word or phrase to represent a possible outcome. Arrange them on the altar before the image of Santa Muerte, make your invocations, then ask your question. Light the candles and observe which one burns down first; whatever was inscribed on it is the answer to your question.

Divination by Means of Candle Wax in Water

To know present conditions that are otherwise unknowable or to know the future, place a brown candle before an image of Santa Muerte, make your usual invocations and ask your question.

Allow the candle to burn, at least, one hour. Then, fill a glass about 3/4 full with clean water and pour the wax into it. Interpret the figures much as you would if you were reading tea leaves. A list of symbols and their meanings are provided further below in this chapter.

Divination by Means of an Egg in Water

The Grimoire of Santa Muerte, Vol.1: Spells and Rituals of Most Holy Death, the Unofficial Saint of Mexico describes a Limpia ritual for cleansing and divining the existence of the Evil Eye, however, Santa Muerte can assist with other types of egg divination, as well.

Place a fresh, uncooked, egg on the altar before an image of Santa Muerte. Light a brown candle to her and make your request: *O Most Holy Death, who knows all and sees all, by means of this egg I ask you to reveal to me _____.*

After an hour has passed, prepare a glass of water as previously described. Remove the egg from the altar, break it and allow its contents to fall into the water. Then, interpret the symbols found in the formations you see there, as described below.

Divination by Ashes

When you burn an item on the altar, observe the remains to determine the outcome of a working or other factors related to the situation. Interpret the symbols that form in the ashes.

Symbols and Their Meaning

Anchor: A beneficial partnership.
Arrow: Bad news.
Bat: Disappointment.

Bell: News; an announcement; if two bells a wedding announcement.

Bird: Important information from an unexpected source.

Boat: Travel by water.

Bubbles: If many bubbles, financial success; if a few bubbles, you will encounter a phase of monetary difficulties.

Car: Mobility; travel; progression of your plans.

Castle: Financial gain through a beneficial union.

Cat: A guardian spirit is nearby.

Chair: An unexpected visitor.

Circle: If whole and unbroken, a good omen; if broken, a sign of betrayal and difficulties. If the circle appears with a dot or bubble in the center, a pregnancy.

Cloak: Protection by Santa Muerte

Clover: Good luck

Coins: If many coins, great financial success; if few coins, a period of financial struggle.

Coffin: Rest, repose; the cessation of difficulties.

Cross: Power; spiritual protection.

Crown: A powerful ally.

Cup: Abundance; happiness; love.

Devil: Bedevilments; annoyances; small troubles.

Door: Santa Muerte has created an opportunity for you; the portal between the physical and spiritual worlds is open.

Dots: If many dots, financial success; if a few dots, you will encounter a phase of monetary difficulties.

Dragon: Drastic changes; an enemy; trouble ahead.

Eye: Spirits are nearby; someone is watching over you; misunderstandings, which will be resolved

Face: An interfering person; if multiple faces, a conspiracy of interference.

Feather: Insubstantial ideas; lack of focus and concentration.

Fish: Good luck.

Flowers: A reminder that Santa Muerte keeps her promises.

Foot: New opportunities; a chance to take your life in a new direction.

Frog or Toad: Transformation; changes; a new job; a new home.

Fork: Flatterer; treacherous friend.

Gate: Santa Muerte is opening the door to new worlds for you; a new opportunity.

Hammer: Destruction of obstacles.

Hand: Someone close to you is in need of help.

Handcuffs: Legal trouble ahead.

Hat: A new career opportunity.

Hen: A happy home.

Heart: Love and compassion.

Horseshoe: If the points are up, good luck, especially in love or finances; if the points are down, protection.

House: Safety; security.

Key: Santa Muerte is opening doors for you; freedom; if two crossed keys, your dreams are realized.

Keyhole: Watch who is watching you.

Ladder: Progress; a promotion at work; financial improvement.

Leaf: Prosperity; abundance; good fortune.

Lines: If straight and unbroken, easy progress; if wavy; difficulties; if jagged, failure.

Lock: An obstacle that must be overcome.

Mountain: Success; obstacles are overcome; projects come to fruition

Mouse: Thief.

Moon: All the blessings of Santa Muerte.

Owl: A warning; hidden danger lurks in the darkness.

Rat: Traitor.

Reptile: Treachery; betrayal.

Revolver: Danger; enemies.

Ring: Engagement; marriage; a partnership. If broken, a broken engagement, divorce, a parting of ways.

Roses: Santa Muerte is by your side.

Scales: A lawsuit. If the scales are balanced, justice will prevail; if the scales are unbalanced, justice will not be served through the courts.

Scythe: Santa Muerte is acting on your behalf.

Ship: A windfall; unexpected rewards.

Skull: Power; Santa Muerte makes all things possible to you.

Snake: An enemy; enmity.

Spider: Secrets; an enemy plotting.

Spoon: Wealth; generosity.

Star: If 4-pointed, a warning of conflict ahead; if 5-pointed, good fortune and a new opportunity; if 6-pointed, health and happiness; if 7-pointed, grief; if 8-pointed, a warning to be careful of accidents.

Sun: Happiness; family; everything associated with success in life.

Sword: Danger is near.

Telephone: Interruption; unwelcome news.

Thorns: Difficulties; conflicts.

Tree: Success.

Trellis: You have a strong relationship with Santa Muerte and are under her protection.

Triangle: Unexpected turn of events; if the point is up, beneficial; if the point is down; detrimental.

Wings: An important letter or message is forthcoming.

Dreams of Santa Muerte

Sometimes people who are not devotees of Santa Muerte have frightening dreams of her or a figure they may identify as the Grim Reaper. She sometimes makes menacing appearances to those who have committed an offense against her children, appearing not only in nightmares, but during waking hours, lurking on the offenders' rooftops or leaping on top of their moving automobiles. Such people are subject to her wrath and will soon experience the justice she brings to a situation.

By contrast, Santa Muerte is always kind and compassionate toward her devoted children who love her. She never harms them and always protects them. So, as a devotee, your dreams of Santa Muerte will always be a comfort to you. Once you have your first dream of her, you will most certainly look forward to seeing her, again. When she appears she often has a message to impart to you.

Sometimes she speaks to you directly, but more often, she communicates through imagery and symbols. If you dream of Santa Muerte three nights in a row, this means there is something she wants you to do for her.

The symbolism in your dreams may correspond to the meanings for various symbols given above for interpreting wax and egg formations. But, more often they will contain a more complex and personal meaning for you. When you have dreams of Santa Muerte, record them and meditate on their meaning for you personally.

To Receive Prophetic Dreams from Santa Muerte

Perform the following ritual to obtain information from Santa Muerte through dreams:

Brown image of Santa Muerte
Brown candle
Brown altar cloth
Flowers
Bay leaves
Mugwort
Lavender
Sachet or small muslin drawstring bag
Bread sprinkled with cinnamon
Seeds
Offerings in the numbers 3

Place three bay leaves and a handful each of dried lavender and mugwort into the sachet or bag and place it on the altar.
Recite the following prayer:

O Most Holy Death, Empress of the Underworld,
Whose powers in both this world and the worlds beyond are infinite,
I ask that you use your holy scythe on my behalf,
To destroy all evil, enmity, and envy, that threatens me,
That you shelter and shield me by the power of your holy cloak,

And that you send your holy companion the owl to advise me.
O Most Holy Death, who knows the secrets of the universe,
I ask that you be my holy guardian and guide,
Tonight, as I dream, appear to me and send spirits to speak to me
To tell me the things I wish to know.
[Insert your petition.]
O Most Holy Death, please, walk beside me all the days of my life.
In the name of the Father, the Son and the Holy Ghost. Amen.

Allow the candles to burn for an hour or so before snuffing them out and retiring to bed. Place the bag filled with herbs beneath your pillow before lying down to sleep. Place a notepad and pen by your bedside so you can record your dreams as soon as you wake.

Divination with Pendulums and Other Devices

Anytime you use a pendulum or similar device to find the answer to a question, make your usual invocations to Santa Muerte and say: *O Most Holy Death, I ask that you let your immense power flow through this instrument; let it always give me right and true answers to my questions.*

You may place any of your divination instruments (e.g., pendulum, dowsing rod, tarot deck, runes) upon the altar for her blessing and make this request during a ritual.

Sharpen your psychic abilities by performing, at least, one Santa Muerte ritual with the brown candle, as described in the previous chapter or at the end of *Chapter 5. Altar Arrangements for Various Purposes with Prayers*, using the altar arrangement for "Psychic Development and Divination Skills."

RITUALS TO DEVELOP YOUR OCCULT POWERS AND ACHIEVE HIGH SPIRITUAL STATES

Santa Muerte can help you along the path of spiritual development through the achievement of high spiritual states, which are consciousness-expanding and transformative, leading to a greater understanding of the occult through personal experience. The prayers and rituals described in this chapter will help you acquire many of the abilities associated with traditional witchcraft.

As always, you may use either the basic altar or an entirely color-coordinated one and appropriate offerings. Since these rituals involve opening mental and spiritual doors, place iron keys on the altar. Begin prayers with your usual invocations and light, at least, one candle.

To Break Mental Programming

Mental programming forms patterns of belief, which can be both illusory and limiting, and constrains your exploration of the occult. This includes ancestral and intergenerational programming. Ancestral programs are the old thought patterns, experiences, and emotions you inherited from your ancestors through genetics. Intergenerational programs involve information you received from your parents about the nature of reality. Other mental programming is social, educational, and religious in nature.

Along your spiritual journey, you will undoubtedly run across information that jars your sensibilities because it is at odds with your conventional education regarding such subjects as history, science, and religion. When new information conflicts with your mental programming, you must release these old, false beliefs to accommodate your new, more accurate perception of reality.

Although you may have rejected some of this harmful mental programming on the conscious level (for example, authoritarianism or old religious beliefs), the subconscious residue may remain even decades later until it is acknowledged and purged. These mental programs contain not only obstructive thought circuits, but corresponding emotional patterns, which function to bind them in place. Both, the thought patterns and the emotions associated with them, must be destroyed in order to fully eradicate the program.

The purpose of the ritual, below, is to help you eliminate old mental programming. Use blue on the altar and make offerings in the numbers 5 or 9. To create a talisman to carry with you, choose a gemstone with the properties to break old programming from *Chapter 3: Gemstone Correspondences to Santa Muerte's Powers*, under the subheading, "Mental Focus and Creativity." Whenever you can identify particular mental programming and associated thought and emotional patterns, which you wish to neutralize, describe them in your petition and ask Santa Muerte to destroy them.

Recite the following prayer:

O Most Holy Death, who knows all and sees all,
Whose powers in both this world and the worlds beyond are infinite,
Cast the light of your holy lamp into the dark corners of my mind,
Use your holy scythe to root out and destroy mental programming,
Which has created illusions, led me to false beliefs about myself and the world,

And is restraining my mind and obstructing my spiritual progress.
I especially ask that you [Insert your petition].
O Blessed Mother, my holy guardian and guide,
I ask that you send your holy companion, the owl,
To whisper in my ear and impart your wisdom,
Shine the light of your holy lamp on all of creation,
That I may break all illusions and see the world around me as it truly is,
That I may come to know myself and my true will.
O Most Holy Death, never forsake me, but be my loving guide, now and forever more.
In the name of the Father, the Son and the Holy Ghost. Amen.

After performing this ritual, be prepared for meaningful dreams at night and synchronous events during your waking hours, which will lead you to illuminating information and sudden epiphanies.

Telepathy

Telepathy is the power to send and receive messages from one mind to another. This ability goes beyond mere intuition, strong feelings, or empathy; it requires an exertion and extension of the mental field to make contact with that of another person. Then, it requires the natural ability to read electromagnetic wave signals in much the same way as the physical eyes and ears read the signals they translate into ordinary sights and sounds. Such communication can take place between two people who are in the same room together or who are a long distance apart.

Choose a stone talisman that is appropriate for telepathy from *Chapter 3: Gemstone Correspondences to Santa Muerte's Powers*, under the subheading, "Spirit Communication, Divination, and E.S.P." Place it on the altar at the feet of an image of Santa Muerte or in her hands. Use brown on the altar and make offerings in the number 3.

Recite the following prayer:

O Most Holy Death, Empress of the Underworld,
Who traverses the many realms beyond the grave,
Nothing is a mystery and all things are possible to you.

I ask that you, please, expand and attune my mental body,
So that I am able to transmit and receive information from the minds of others.
I ask that you lay your powerful hand upon this stone,
Let it become an instrument of your great power,
So that whenever I carry it with me, I automatically have telepathic abilities.
[Insert your petition.]
In the name of the Father, the Son and the Holy Ghost. Amen.

Meditate with this stone and carry it with you as a talisman whenever you want to perform telepathy. After you do this for a while, your mental body will become reconfigured and you will no longer need the talisman.

To Communicate with Animals, Birds, and Insects

Communicating with animals, birds, and insects is similar to telepathy between human minds. Perform the following ritual to acquire the ability to send and receive communications, establish rapport, and command them.

Follow the same procedure as for telepathy, above, using a different stone talisman. Use brown on the altar and make offerings in the number 3.

Recite the following prayer:

O Most Holy Death, Empress of the Underworld,
Who traverses the many realms beyond the grave,
Nothing is a mystery and all things are possible to you.
I ask that you, please, expand and attune my mental body,
So that I am able to transmit and receive information,
Mind to mind and spirit to spirit.
Let me communicate with all animals, birds, and insects,
So that they shall understand me, provide me with information,
And, when requested, do as I bid.
I ask that you lay your powerful hand upon this stone,
So that it shall, from this moment on, serve as an instrument of your

power,
   So that whenever I carry it with me, I automatically have this ability.
   [Insert your petition.]
   In the name of the Father, the Son and the Holy Ghost. Amen.

Meditate with this stone and carry it with you whenever you wish to communicate with animals. After a while, the ability will come very naturally to you.

The Awareness and Control of Subtle Energy

The human body is a microcosm of the universe, therefore, awareness and control of your own subtle energy fields constitute the initial step to a greater understanding of how all witchcraft works. The following rituals concern these subtle fields and the related bodies, which are spiritual vehicles of the human consciousness.

For all of the following rituals use the color purple on your altar and make offerings in the numbers 7 or 12. See *Chapter 3: Gemstone Correspondences to Santa Muerte's Powers*, under the subheading, "Occult Powers and High Spiritual States," to select an appropriate gemstone for meditation and talisman-creation.

Invisibility

Invisibility is achieved when the human body's etheric emanations are prevented from reaching the human eye. The etheric body sends out waves of energy or light rays, which are perceived by others as visible images. If these rays are returned to the body, they cannot be perceived by others and the physical body's presence will be imperceptible.

To go about unseen, acquire a bloodstone, consecrate it to this sole purpose, and regularly meditate with it by holding it in your right hand as you repeat, either silently or aloud, the following Latin phrase: Revertere meis lucem. (Ray-vare-tay-ray may-ees loo-sem) Meaning: Return my light.

Consecrate the bloodstone on the altar by placing it at the feet of Santa Muerte and reciting the following prayer:

O Most Holy Death, Empress of the Underworld,
Who knows the secrets of the universe,
I ask that you lay your hand upon this stone,
That, henceforth, it shall be an instrument of your power.
By the medium of this stone, return the light waves to me,
So that they cannot be perceived and I may pass unseen.
[Insert your petition.]
In the name of the Father, the Son and the Holy Ghost. Amen.

Keep the bloodstone with you as a talisman and whenever you wish to render yourself invisible, turn it three times clockwise while reciting the Latin meditation above. To be seen and acknowledged, again, turn the stone three times counterclockwise.

True Perceptions

If you wish to see the world and everyone in it as they really are, ask Santa Muerte to help you increase your awareness by expanding your personal frequency range so that you are able to receive and interpret signals from the astral, etheric, and mental planes. To see the world and everything in it as it really is, without illusion or glamour, perform this ritual.

Choose a unakite gemstone to be your talisman. Place it on the altar before Santa Muerte or in one of her hands.

Then, recite the following prayer:

O Most Holy Death, Empress of the Underworld,
Who knows all and sees all, I know that nothing is a mystery to you.
I ask that by the power of your holy scythe,
You rend the veil between the worlds
And destroy the illusions of this earthly existence.
O Most Holy Death, please, lay your hand upon this stone
That, henceforth, it shall be an instrument of your power,
By which I cannot be deceived and the true nature
Of all things shall at once be revealed to me.
[Insert your petition.]
In the name of the Father, the Son and the Holy Ghost. Amen.

When the candle has burned down, collect the stone, meditate with it, and carry it with you to activate this latent ability.

Telekinesis

Telekinesis is the ability to move objects at a distance by the power of the mind. Some forms of healing are accomplished by means of telekinesis, such as manipulating energy fields to heal injured tissues or using magnetism to manipulate organs of the body. Many famous examples of of telekinesis are documented in the book, *Psychic Discoveries Behind the Iron Curtain*, by Sheila Ostrander, Lynn Schroeder, which was first published in 1970.

Contrary to popular perception, it is not accomplished by "mind over matter," but rather by exerting the force of the mental body (the will) onto the etheric field of an object. Perform a ritual

to Santa Meurte to activate your latent telekinetic power.
Recite the following prayer:

O Most Holy Death, Empress of the Underworld,
Who knows the mysteries of the universe,
By the light of your holy lamp, illuminate my path,
Reveal to me the truth about the natural world,
Let nothing be a mystery to me,
Bless me with the ability to focus and learn,
So that may easily develop my latent telekinetic abilities.
Bless me with an abundance of personal energy,
Mental force and persistence of will.
[Insert your petition.]
O Most Holy Death, be my my holy guide and mentor,
Never leave my side, but be with me now and forever more.
In the name of the Father, the Son and the Holy Ghost. Amen.

To create a talisman, choose tunellite or another gemstone with properties that support telekinesis. Meditate with this stone, place it on the altar during your rituals for this purpose, and keep it with you whenever you wish to practice this skill.

Consciousness Transference

Consciousness transference is an out-of-body experience in which you project your consciousness outside your physical body and into an object, animal, or plant. Mastery of this skill, is the first step in being able to exercise a more sophisticated degree of control over the consciousness and the subtle bodies.

To practice consciousness transference, allow yourself to become very relaxed while in a seated position. Choose an object, such as a chair or vase, and move your awareness into it so that you become as one with it. Once you have moved your consciousness to this place, look out on the room from its perspective. After you practice this technique with non-living things, move on to plants and then insects, birds, and animals.

To obtain Santa Muerte's assistance, perform a ritual for this purpose, in which you recite the following prayer:

O Most Holy Death, Almighty Mother of All
Who knows the secrets of the universe,
I ask that, by the power of your holy scythe,
You rend the veil between the worlds
And destroy the illusions of this earthly existence.
When I will it, let me leave my body and enter another form,
And ensure that I can instantly return to my body at will.
[Insert your petition.]
O Most Holy Death, My holy guardian and dearest friend,
I trust in you and I know that you will always keep me safe
I ask that you never leave my side, now and forever more.
In the name of the Father, the Son and the Holy Ghost. Amen.

To create a talisman, choose a gemstone with properties that support out-of-body experiences. Meditate with this stone, place it on the altar during your rituals for this purpose, and keep it with you whenever you wish to practice this skill.

Astral Projection

Astral projection is an out-of-body experience similar to consciousness transference, except that you direct your consciousness into your astral body, instead of transferring it into an object or other physical form. The astral realm is characterized by emotions and occupied by a variety of spirits, including demons, angels, discarnate human souls, and elemental beings. Astral travel is akin to lucid dreaming in which the dreamer's experiences are especially vivid and realistic.

To activate and refine your latent ability to project your consciousness into your astral body and explore the astral realm at will, perform a ritual to Santa Muerte for this purpose, in which you recite the following prayer:

> O Most Holy Death, Empress of the Underworld,
> Who knows the secrets of the universe,
> I ask that by the power of your holy scythe,
> You rend the veil between the worlds
> And destroy the illusions of this earthly existence.
> Reveal the mysteries that lay beyond the grave,
> Let me know other worlds and the secrets of the dead and discarnate.
> I now ask that you free me from all worldly cares and concerns
> And release my consciousness from my physical body into my astral body.
> I have no fear of leaving my body because
> I know you will be with me, your holy lamp will guide me,
> With your holy cloak you will shield me from all evil,
> And just as I will leave my body as I choose,
> I will just as easily return the instant I desire it.
> [Insert your petition.]
> O Most Holy Death, be my holy guardian and guide,
> Never leave my side, but be with me every step, now and forever more.
> In the name of the Father, the Son and the Holy Ghost. Amen.

Repeat this prayer whenever you practice astral projection by means of meditation or to induce lucid dreaming before falling asleep. To create a talisman, choose a gemstone with properties that support astral projection. Meditate with this stone, place it on the altar during your rituals for this purpose, and keep it with you whenever you wish to practice this skill.

Bilocation

Bilocation is the ability to be in two places at the same time. To accomplish this, you must extrude your astral and etheric bodies to produce a large accumulation of dense etheric energy, from which to generate an exact copy of your etheric body. This second etheric body, which can be projected to a distant location, is formative to the new dense physical body, which is only temporary. You must, then, transfer your consciousness into this new form. It requires a great deal of power combined with the directed will to create a copy of the physical body.

To activate your latent ability to bilocate, enter a relaxed, meditative, and highly focused state. Then, perform a ritual to Santa Muerte for this purpose, in which you recite the following prayer:

O Most Holy Death, Empress of the Underworld,
Who knows the secrets of the universe,
I ask that by the power of your holy scythe,
You rend the veil between the worlds
And destroy the illusions of this earthly existence.
Reveal to me the mysteries of all the saints and spiritual masters.
Grant me the knowledge and power
To unlock my latent ability to bilocate.
When I will it, extrude my vital force to form a new etheric body,
Out of which to form a new physical body,
And let me easily transfer my consciousness
To my new form, so I can go wherever I need to go
And do whatever I need to do in the physical world.
Let nothing harm me on my journey.
When I wish to return, dissolve my temporary form
And ensure my quick and safe return to my mundane body.
[Insert your petition.]
O Most Holy Death, be my holy guardian and guide,
Never leave my side, but be with me every step, now and forever more.
In the name of the Father, the Son and the Holy Ghost. Amen.

When you wish to practice bilocation, go into a deeply meditative state and recite this prayer to Santa Muerte. To create a talisman, choose a gemstone with properties that support bilocation. Meditate with this stone, place it on the altar during your rituals, and keep it with you whenever you wish to practice this skill.

Always perform bilocation and transmogrification, which is described below, in a safe environment in which your dense physical body will remain at rest and undisturbed. The projection of the etheric body, such as occurs during bilocation and transmogrification is very similar to the projection of ectoplasm by a spiritualist medium. According to a large body of spiritualist research, any disturbance of the physical body during the projection of etheric matter, can result in injury and possibly even death.

Transmogrification or Shape-shifting

In Mexico, "nahual," (pronounced Na-wal), also spelled "nagual," is another name for a witch, especially one who can transmogrify or shift into other forms, such as birds, cats, and nocturnal creatures. Transmogrification allows you to perform tasks that would otherwise be difficult or impossible and to pass unrecognized. Witches who practice transmogrification use it to perform healing, rescue people in trouble, obtain revenge, and perform other occult work.

Transmogrification is similar to the practice of bilocation except that instead of projecting an exact copy of the etheric body, you form one that takes on different characteristics. The changes you make in your projected etheric body, will be reflected in your new, temporary physical body. It is not always desirable to completely assume the shape of an animal, but to borrow certain characteristics, such as wings, claws, or fangs, and combine these with your own. The practice of telepathically communicating with animals supports the development of the ability to transmogrify by helping you to establish a rapport with creatures whose characteristics you want to borrow.

To activate your latent ability to transmogrify, enter a relaxed, meditative, and highly focused state. Then, perform a ritual to Santa Muerte for this purpose, in which you recite the following prayer:

O Most Holy Death, Queen of the Night,
Who knows the secrets of the universe,
I ask that by the power of your holy scythe,
You rend the veil between the worlds
And destroy the illusions of this earthly existence.
By the power of your holy lamp, illuminate the night,
And reveal to me the oldest, most guarded secrets
Of the witches who came before me,
Which are shrouded in nocturnal mystery.
Bring this obscure knowledge forth out of the darkness to me.
Grant me the knowledge and power
To unlock my latent ability to transmogrify.
When I will it, extrude my vital force to form a new etheric body,
Let the changes in my form, which I desire,
Take place at the moment I will it to be so.
And let me easily transfer my consciousness
To my new physical form, so I can go wherever I need to go
And do whatever I need to do in the physical world.
Let nothing harm me on my journey.
When I wish to return, dissolve my temporary form
And ensure my quick and safe return to my mundane body.
[Insert your petition.]
O Most Holy Death, be my my holy guardian and guide,
Never leave my side, but be with me every step, now and forever more.
In the name of the Father, the Son and the Holy Ghost. Amen.

When you wish to practice transmogrification, go into a deeply meditative state, visualize in minute detail the form you wish to take, and recite this prayer to Santa Muerte. To create a talisman, choose a gemstone with properties that support transmogrification. Black obsidian is the classic stone for this purpose. Meditate with it, place it on the altar during your rituals, and keep it with you whenever you wish to practice this skill.

Take care of your safety while transmogrified and ensure that your resting physical body will remain completely undisturbed during the course of your travels.

Give Thanks to Santa Muerte for Her Assistance

Whenever you succeed, feed Santa Muerte's power at your altar by giving her thanks and praise. Make copious, powerful offerings to her and express your sincere gratitude to her for the gifts she has given you.

Recite the following prayer:

O Most Holy Death, Most Powerful Mother of All,
I place these offerings before you in gratitude
For the many gifts you have granted me.
At times of great sorrow, you have comforted me.
When I have been sick and tired, you have healed and rejuvenated me.
When I have faced terrible enemies, you have protected me.
At the time of my greatest need, you have provided for me.
You have opened doors to mysteries that were once closed to me
And given new meaning to my life.
I will praise your holy name all the days of my life.
I ask that you continue to bless me with your infinite compassion.
[Insert your petition.]
O Most Holy Death, grant me peace and protection,
Never leave my side, but always be my holy guide, now and forever more.
In the name of the Father, the Son and the Holy Ghost. Amen.

RITUALS AND TALISMANS TO INFLUENCE THE WEATHER

Control of the weather involves an exertion of the will, by means of the mental body, directed onto the etheric fields of the natural elements. Santa Muerte can provide you with the necessary power and assist you in developing this ability.

In each of the following rituals, a procedure for weather control is encoded into a talisman, which is set aside solely for that purpose. Arrange your altar using the colors purple or black and make offerings in the numbers 4 or 12.

To Control the Rain

For the purposes of bringing rain and restoring clear skies, acquire a bloodstone as a talisman. Consecrate it to this sole purpose and regularly meditate with it by holding the stone in your right hand as you repeat, either silently or aloud, the following Latin phrase: *Verte radiis solis.* (Vare-tay rad-ees sol-ees) Meaning: Turn the rays of the sun.

To consecrate the bloodstone, place it before the image of Santa Muerte or in one of her hands, then recite the following prayer:

O Most Holy Death,
You who holds the earth in your hands,
Who has knowledge of and power over the elements,
I place this stone before you for you to lay you hand upon it
Please, give it your blessing that it shall henceforth
Be an instrument of your holy power.
In the name of the Father, the Son and the Holy Ghost. Amen.

Collect the stone, place it in a little cloth bag until you're ready to use it.

To Bring the Rain

When skies are clear and you want to bring rain or a storm, turn the holy bloodstone three times while reciting the Latin meditation above, "*Verte radiis solis.*" Then, place it in a glass of water on the altar.

Recite the following prayer:

O Most Holy Death,
By the power of your holy scythe,
I ask that you draw the clouds up in a bundle,
Knit them tightly together and warm them,
Then, let rain pour forth,
In the name of the Father, the Son and the Holy Ghost. Amen.

To Restore Clear Skies

To restore clear skies, remove the stone from the water, again, turn it three times while reciting the same Latin phrase, then place it on a window sill and allow it to dry.

After you have successfully performed the ritual to bless the stone and brought rain and restored clear skies several times, you may carry the stone with you to control the weather wherever you go. Simply turn the stone three times while reciting the meditation, "*Verte radiis solis*," then recite the prayer to bring the rain or restore clear skies.

To Control the Wind

To control the wind, create a talisman consecrated to Santa Muerte as instructed below.

To create the cord, you will need the following items:

- A length of cord 1/8" to 1/4" (approximately .3 to .65 cm) in diameter and between 18" and 24" (approximately 45 to 60 cm) long.
- 4 beads with a whole large enough to pass the cord through in the following colors: Black; white; red and blue.
- 9 feathers

Let the blue bead represent the north wind; the white bead represent the south wind; the red bead represent the east wind; and the black bead represent the west wind.

Each of the nine feathers will represents the power and strength of the winds.

In all there will be 13 knots, each made around a feather or through a bead so it can be easily loosened.

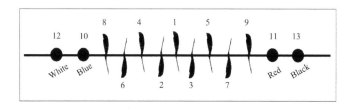

Go before your altar with your cord, beads and feathers. Make your usual invocations, light and candle and create the talisman, as follows:

Place a feather in the center of the cord, then tie a knot around it as you say: *By the power of Most Holy Death, I hereby constrain and harness the forces that breathe gales, gusts, and cyclones over the earth.*

Tie each of the next 8 knots the same way, making them far enough apart that the knots can be loosened, and working your way out away from the first knot, first one side of the center knot and then on the other side so they are as evenly spaced as possible.

Then, tie the blue bead (the 10th knot) a distance away from the last feather on one side of the cord and, as you tie the knot, say: *By the power of Most Holy Death, I hereby bind the spirit of the north wind.*

On the opposite end, tie the red bead (the 11th knot) a distance away from the last feather as you say: *By the power of Most Holy Death, I hereby bind the spirit of the east wind.*

Then, at the opposite end of the cord, near the blue bead, tie the white one (the 12th knot) as you say: *By the power of Most Holy Death, I hereby bind the spirit of the south wind.*

Then, at the other end of the cord, again, next to the red bead, tie the black one (the 13th knot) as you say: *By the power of Most Holy Death, I hereby bind the spirit of the west wind.*

Then, wrap the knotted cord around the base of the image of Santa Muerte, or place it in her hands and recite the following prayer:

O Most Holy Death,
You who holds the earth in your hands,
Who has knowledge of and power over the elements,
I place talisman before you for you to lay you hand upon it.
Please, give it your blessing that it shall henceforth
Be an instrument of your holy power,
So that by means of it, I control the force and direction of the winds.
In the name of the Father, the Son and the Holy Ghost. Amen.

Allow the cord to remain on the altar until the candle burns down. Once every three weeks, place the cord on the altar before Santa Muerte or in her hands and repeat this prayer, again, to infuse ever greater power into the talisman.

How to Use the Talisman To Raise and Direct the Wind

To raise and direct the winds, call upon the power of Santa Muerte as you remove particular knots in the cord.

Light a candle, then recite the following prayer:

O Most Holy Death, Empress of the Underworld,
I know that by your hand all things are possible.
At this time, I call upon your infinite power
Over the forces of nature.
As I loosen these knots, release the winds.
As I bind them, calm the gales, again,
In accordance with my will.
[Insert your petition.]
In the name of the Father, the Son and the Holy Ghost. Amen.

When you want to raise wind, untie one knot for each degree of strength. To determine the intensity of the force of the wind, loosen the knotted feathers for greater force, beginning with the center knot and working your way out evenly (loosen the first knot, then the second and third, up to the ninth.)

To direct the wind, loosen the one or more of the directional beads. For instance, for a strong wind out of the west, loosen the black bead and its knot. For a southwestern wind, loosen both the black and white beads.

For destructive winds, untie most or all of the knots.

To restore calm, tighten the knots, again. Then, fasten the cord around the base of an image of Santa Muerte on your altar.

To cause a storm at a particular location or at a particular time, insert this request into your petition to Santa Muerte. Loosen the knots according to your desire. To restore calm, tighten the knots.

Sophia diGregorio

TRANSCENDENCE: ENCOURAGEMENT
AND A WARNING

When some of the rituals, meditations, and prayers in this book
are performed in earnest, they are a means of transcendence with
the assistance of Santa Muerte. Transcendence means going
beyond the mundane physical world, becoming something other
than the mere sophisticated animals that humans are supposed to
be, according to orthodox science. With respect to this outcome, it
is appropriate to provide a few final instructions, a warning, and
some encouragement for you to persevere on this course of
discovery.

Reading a book about a subject provides you with knowledge
by means of information, ideas, inspiration, and instruction,
however, true knowledge of the occult can only come from
personal experience. This is achieved through experimentation and
incremental mastery of the concepts presented herein. It begins
with becoming increasingly aware of subtle energy and learning to
direct it, practicing meditation to achieve particular goals, mastering
the power of the altar, and the use of ritual.

Sophia diGregorio

Your experiences will take you beyond the supposed limitations of the material world. Beginning with the first few steps, you will move ever further beyond your present level of attainment, as you will it.

Why Pursue Occult Knowledge

Many people who express an interest in the occult do so because they have already had a transcendent experience. Common examples of these experiences include such things as clairaudience, clairvoyance, and telekinesis. Because of these personal experiences, they already know that something is wrong with the official story — the official science, the official history, the society as a whole and the beliefs of most of the people in it. What most people don't know, especially in the beginning, is just how wrong it all is. But, it is this first inkling that spurs questions about the true nature of the world.

The quest to find the answers becomes an unremitting pursuit of the truth, wherever it takes you. If you pursue this course very far, you will advance beyond the material world, transforming yourself, your life, and your view of the world and everything and everyone in it. Only when you know the truth can you determine your own true will and fulfill your life's purpose.

Along the way, you will acquire occult abilities that are useful in this life. The quest leads to the liberation of the mind, which leads to greater freedom in the physical world, since you learn to do many things that are regarded as either unusual or impossible by most people. Knowledge truly is power and occult knowledge is occult power.

How to Uncover What is Hidden with the Help of Santa Muerte

In order to discover the truth, it is often necessary to first destroy lies. This is why one of the most important rituals in this book is the one called "To Break Mental Programming," at the beginning of *Chapter 8. Rituals to Develop Your Occult Powers and*

Achieve High Spiritual States. The other rituals in this chapter help to develop your occult powers, ultimately allowing you to move freely between the worlds of the living and the dead in much the same way as Santa Muerte does. Mental programming is a prison of the mind and each of these rituals holds a key to freedom.

Repeat the ritual, "To Break Mental Programming," often. Meditate on this goal and reflect deeply on your own beliefs; examine what you believe and why you believe it. Petition Santa Muerte to help you identify and break programming. Ask her to illuminate the darkness by the power of her holy lamp so you can see what is hidden and find your path; to use the power of her holy scythe to rend the veil between the worlds and destroy illusions; and to dispatch her owl to you to give you guidance, wisdom, and information. Ask her to send other spirits to inform you, as you require. She can send you not only spirits of the dead, but ancient spirits who have never had the human experience.

Mental programming goes back to very early childhood and even beyond since human beings, also, have ancestral programming, sometimes called "genetic memory" or "racial memory", which creates emotional responses and thought processes that may not be your own, but are inherited from your ancestors. Mental programming is layered, one concept on top of another. Removing one layer almost always reveals another.

Mental programs appear as truths too obvious to question. The more natural, unquestioned, absolute, accepted, commonplace, and innate an idea seems, the more you should challenge it. The hallmark of mental programming is authoritarianism. You are made to believe something because an authority, such as a priest, a scientist, a doctor, a teacher, or a parent, said so. Question all authority, all institutions, and all doctrines. Question all commonly accepted beliefs.

Be single-minded in your pursuit of occult knowledge. Ask Santa Muerte for mental focus and to lead you to the information you require. Answers to questions should always be your own, arrived at after deliberation. Let your own rational observations and experiences be your guide, rather than faith or belief in something simply because it is a popular belief or an authority figure said so.

Seek a secluded place to reflect for long periods of time, for weeks or months, if possible, to eliminate external influences. Ideally, get to an ocean or to mountains and away from "civilization." If this is not possible, at least, do not expose yourself to television and popular media. If you get away from these influences for very long, your mind will experience a natural cleansing and, afterward, you may find that it is very difficult to return to them. Once liberated, the mind strongly resists returning to a mental prison.

Writing is one of the best ways to break free of repressive thought patterns and to get at the truth. Keep a journal to record your observations, experiences, and conclusions and as a record of your personal journey into the occult.

Personal experiences with such things as subtle energy manipulation, divination, out-of-body-experiences, and manipulation of weather events, also, break old mental programming by forcing you to acknowledge that the world does not work the way you were probably led to believe it does.

A Warning

Venturing far into the occult can be fraught with difficulties or, at least, discomfort for a number of reasons. When the illusions of the dense physical world begin to fade away, you may have trouble connecting with other people who do not have the same perceptions. As a result, you may begin to feel alienated and alone, although, there are many people who know the truth.

There is, also, the difficulty of completely controlling your heightened sensory abilities. Being able to read the thoughts and emotions of other people and knowing the true spiritual nature of some human beings, although enlightening, can be frightening at times. This is one of the reasons that people with highly developed psychic abilities, wise women and men, often live in isolation away from civilization.

Breaking mental programming often involves the release of negative emotions. When the thought loop is broken, the emotions attached to it will be released, too. You may begin to remember unpleasant events from childhood. Some of what is uncovered may be traumatic memories, which have been buried to protect the mind and emotions. Sometimes this can cause intense dreams or nightmares.

This undertaking may prove too difficult or even inadvisable, especially for people who are in committed relationships, because going very far in this process can completely alter not only perceptions, but sometimes a person's personality may change as a result of mental deprogramming and transformational occult experiences. Furthermore, once mental programming is broken, it cannot be re-constructed. You will have to live with the knowledge you have acquired.

Encouragement

Once you have begun your journey into the occult experience, you may find that there is really no option but to continue further into transcendence. At a certain point in this process, breaking the mental programming becomes enjoyable and the acquisition of new knowledge and abilities becomes its own reward. Whatever difficulties you face in your pursuit of occult knowledge, if you persevere, you will find it is worth the effort.

With every new illusion-shattering experience, you are better able to determine your will, free of thoughts and emotions that are not your own. This knowledge eventually leads to peace of mind and a degree of freedom most people find unimaginable. Liberating your mind from mental programming truly frees your will. It expands your mental body, which is the center of all operations in both the physical and metaphysical worlds.

One of the most liberating areas of occult study is that of healing. Performing healing with the assistance of Santa Muerte provides an opportunity to speed up your spiritual progress, gain more experience generating and directing energy, and become more confident in your rapidly developing abilities. Learning to heal the physical and metaphysical bodies is a way to become more independent and self-reliant.

The human body's subtle fields, intelligent entities, healing procedures, rituals, and remedies for healing are discussed in the next volume in this series, *Grimoire of Santa Muerte, Volume 3: Rituals and Remedies for Healing with Most Holy Death*. You will learn that metaphysical theories are not without a foundation in the rational, thus completely breaking down the false mental programming of the scientific orthodoxy, large portions of which are a mental prison. Learning to heal with Santa Muerte is the key to opening more doors to the occult world.

Basic Color Associations of Santa Muerte

Amber: Healing; to break bad habits and addictions

Black: Strength; power; to dispel evil; total protection against enemies; hexing; revenge and to free prisoners

Blue: Wisdom; increased mental powers; creativity and concentration

Bone: Peace and harmony in the home

Brown: Spirit communication; to locate lost objects; divination and protection of family pets

Copper: Exorcism; to remove evil spirits

Gold: Abundance; wealth; power; success and good fortune

Green: Contracts; legal matters; courts; justice and unity

Orange: Cleansing and healing

Purple: Transformation; high spiritual states; to remove obstacles; impossible cases; psychic manifestations; esoteric knowledge and power

Red: Love; romance; passion and protection from evil

Silver: Good luck and success

White: Protection; peace and harmony in the home; loyalty; health and healing of children

Yellow: Good luck; learning; intellectual pursuits and wisdom

Offerings to Santa Muerte

Alcoholic Beverages: Tequila, rum or whiskey placed in a shot glass are common offerings to give power to your workings. Santa Muerte, also, likes dark red wines and dark beers.

Baked Goods: Share cookies, cakes, breads and muffins with her, especially those you have made with your own hands. These are typical offerings for peace in the home, to ward off poverty, for protection of the family and to ask for your needs to be met.

Candles: Candles in various colors are a basic offering to Santa Muerte. Offer her colored candles in accordance with the purpose of your working. If in doubt, choose white. The candle represents the passage of spirits into eternity. A candle placed in a coffin is a symbol of immortality. The flame of the candle carries your communication to the Underworld.

Candy: Offer her sweets, specially cinnamon candy for love, passion and expeditiousness. Chocolate is an ancient offering to the spirits in Mexico, it is especially used for matters pertaining to love and dispelling negativity.

Coffee: Place a small cup of coffee on her altar for energy and to speed a working.

Coins and Paper Currency: Coins of gold, silver and copper and paper currency are offered to her for success in business, money, wealth and success.

Flowers: Fresh flowers are symbolic of the transient and fleeting nature of life. Dyed flowers, including black roses, as well as dried and artificial flowers may be used. Roses and violets are among the most common flowers offered to her. Red roses are for love and passion. White roses, with the thorns removed, are for peace and healing. Offer her flowers for whatever you seek, peace, happiness, spiritual enlightenment, knowledge and transformation.

Fruit: Bowls and cornucopias filled with fresh fruit and vegetables are common offerings. In Mexico, tropical fruits are commonly used, but you may use anything you have. Red apples sprinkled with cinnamon and brown sugar are commonly used in rituals for love, strength, passion, success and financial help. Yellow apples are best for healing and prosperity. Green apples may be used for legal matters.

Gemstones: Offer her quartz crystals and other gemstones in accordance with the purpose of your working. The stones may be placed in water upon the altar.

Herbs: Copal resin is traditionally burned to conjure spirits of all kinds. Frankincense, Myrrh and Juniper are, also, frequently used as offerings. Sage, particularly White Sage, is burned for purification, cleansing and protection from evil. Other herbs are offered in accordance with their metaphysical properties. While fresh herbs may be placed on the altar as an offering, it is common to burn dried herbs as incense. Incense in the form of cones and sticks is, also, a common offering to Santa Muerte.

Honey: Offer her honey to sweeten and strengthen relationships.

Marijuana: Similar to tobacco, below.

Salt: Place a small dish of salt on the altar to energize any working. Salt is, also, used for purification. The salt that is placed on your Santa Muerte altar may be later sprinkled around your home or business or a pinch carried with you to ward off evil spirits and bad people.

Tobacco: Burning tobacco as a means of making contact with spirits is an ancient North American Indian practice. Use tobacco in any form for healing, purification, to dispel envy and to make a spiritual connection. Blow smoke over the altar to purify it. Blow smoke into the face of Santa Muerte as an offering and to make a spiritual connection with her. You may use two cigars or cigarettes as an offering by smoking one and leaving the other for Santa Muerte.

Tortillas: Corn and flour tortillas are traditional offerings to Santa Muerte and other folk saints for promoting the life force and prosperity.

Water: A glass of fresh, clean water is a primary offering to the spirit. A fresh vessel of water should always be present on the altar.

MORE WINTER TEMPEST BOOKS

If you enjoyed this book, you might enjoy other Winter Tempest Books:

All Natural Dental Remedies: Herbs and Home Remedies to Heal Your Teeth & Naturally Restore Tooth Enamel by Angela Kaelin

Black Magic for Dark Times: Spells of Revenge and Protection by Angela Kaelin

The Devil's Grimoire: A System of Psychic Attack by Moribus Mortlock

Grimoire of Santa Muerte: Spells and Rituals of Most Holy Death, the Unofficial Saint of Mexico (Santa Muerte Series) (Volume 1) by Sophia diGregorio

How to Communicate with Spirits: Séances, Ouija Boards and Summoning by Angela Kaelin

How to Develop Advanced Psychic Abilities: Obtain Information about the Past, Present and Future Through Clairvoyance by Sophia diGregorio

How to Read the Tarot for Fun, Profit and Psychic Development for Beginners and Advanced Readers by Angela Kaelin

How to Write Your Own Spells for Any Purpose and Make Them Work by Sophia diGregorio

Magical Healing: How to Use Your Mind to Heal Yourself and Others by Angela Kaelin

Natural Remedies for Reversing Gray Hair: Nutrition and Herbs for Anti-aging and Optimum Health by Thomas W. Xander

Practical Black Magic: How to Hex and Curse Your Enemies by Sophia diGregorio

Spells for Money and Wealth by Angela Kaelin

The Traditional Witches' Book of Love Spells by Angela Kaelin

Traditional Witches' Formulary and Potion-making Guide: Recipes for Magical Oils, Powders and Other Potions by Sophia diGregorio

What's Next After Wicca? Non-Wiccan Occult Practices and Traditional Witchcraft by Sophia diGregorio

Please, visit Winter Tempest Books (http://wintertempestbooks.webs.com) for more occult books and other works by this author.

DISCLAIMER

The author and publisher of this guide has used her best efforts in preparing this document. The author makes no representation or warranties with respect to the accuracy, applicability, fitness or completeness of the contents of this document. The author disclaims any warranties expressed or implied. The author of this book is not a medical or legal professional and is not qualified to give medical or legal advice. Nothing in this document should be construed as medical or legal advice. The material in this book is presented for informational purposes only. The procedures described in this book should not be used a substitute for treatment from state approved, licensed medical authorities.

Nothing in this book should be construed as incitement to dangerous or illegal acts and the reader is advised to be aware of and heed all pertinent laws in his or her city, state, country or other jurisdiction. Any medical or legal questions should be addressed to the proper medical or legal authorities. The author shall in no event be held liable for any losses or damages, including but not limited to special, incidental, consequential or other damages incurred by the use of this information. Always take proper precautions with candles, sharp objects, essential oils, herbs and use only as directed.

The statements in this book have not been evaluated by any other government entity. The statements contained herein represent the legally protected opinions of the author and are presented for informational purposes only. Anyone who uses any of the information in the book does so at their own risk with the understanding that the author cannot be held responsible for the consequences.

FTC Disclaimer: The author has no connection to nor was paid by any brand or product described in this document with the exception of any other books mentioned which were written by the author or published by Winter Tempest Books.

Copyright: This document contains material protected under copyright laws. Any unauthorized reprint, transmission or resale of this material without the express permission of the author is strictly prohibited.

Printed in Great Britain
by Amazon